ELEMENTS

OF

ENCOUNTER

WILLIAM C. SCHUTZ

JOY press

BIG SUR CALIFORNIA 93920

Cover Designed by Susan Stafford

TABLE OF CONTENTS

INTRODUCTION

The encounter group made a dramatic appearance on the American scene in the late 1960's. Newspaper and magazine articles, television appearances, public lectures, and finally a flood of books trumpeted the advent of something new. The prestige of Carl Rogers propelled encounter into the academic world, and his comment that encounter is perhaps the most significant social invention of this century has been quoted so often that it has worn thin.

Encounter is, of course, not new. It has a long and honorable history, both remote and recent. The initial exuberant response to encounter has subsided. Encounter is now experiencing a period of transmutation, and it seems the appropriate time to take a more dispassionate look at what it is, what it is becoming, and how it fits into the nature of things.

This book began with a letter from Raymond Corsini asking me to write a chapter for a book he was editing, *Current Psychotherapies* (Corsini, in press). I complied and liked the result. Following his systematic outline forced me to solidify my writing on encounter: I had to think more about the underlying theory, read relevant research, make my methods explicit, explore historical roots, and generally fill in the gaps in the background of the field and make clearer the things I had just intuited. Buoyed by Corsini's encouraging reception, I decided to expand my chapter and publish it separately.

My earlier books on encounter, *Joy* and *Here Comes Everybody*, describe techniques and my personal evolution in more detail. The present book is my most recent, most concise, and most complete statement of how I see encounter. It is suitable for courses in psychotherapy, clinical psychology, social psychology, education, nursing, religion, administration, sociology, and perhaps for classes in other fields. It may also be useful as a handbook for persons leading or participating in encounter groups, and of help to

1

interested lay persons who simply want to know what encounter is all about.

My appreciation to Corsini for his outline and editorial assistance, to Peacock for permission to expand this chapter into a separate publication, and to Ken Dychtwald, Ralph Colb, and Valerie Blalock for a superb job of editing.

Will Schutz
Big Sur, California
November, 1972

A Note on Style

Standard English grammar and accepted usage have, built into them, certain values, habits of thought, and expectations. Some of these are incompatible with my own values, habits of thought, and expectations and with those of the encounter culture. In instances of manifest conflict, I have followed my own preference at the expense of convention.

I would feel mildly absurd, for example, making third person impersonal generalizations when speaking about myself and my experience, while, at the same time, admonishing you to take responsibility for yourself. These are my words; in the course of this book I often express them in the first person. I often address you, the reader, in the second person. *I* speak to *you.* Especially in the sections dealing with the rules of encounter, principles of encounter, and with phases of group development, it seemed most natural to assume a dialectic interaction between myself, the leader-lecturer, and you, the reader and all-purpose group member. At other times, as when speaking of individual physiological and personality types, it seemed clearer for me to play the universal self and to speak as "I".

Another conflict between encounter culture and English grammar concerns the generic masculine pronoun. "He" is to represent both "he" and "she," "man" to represent both male and female members of the species. New, graceful, accepted conventions are needed — especially pronouns to denote persons of either gender. I have, throughout, done the best I could to preserve clarity and felicity of expression while, at the same time, uniformly eliminating generic masculine usages.

DEFINITION OF ENCOUNTER

Encounter is a method of human relating based on openness and honesty, self-awareness, self-responsibility, awareness of the body, attention to feelings, and an emphasis on the here-and-now. It usually occurs in a group setting. Encounter is therapy insofar as it focuses on removing blocks to better functioning. Encounter is education and recreation in that it attempts to create conditions leading to the most satisfying use of personal capacities.

Encounter usually takes place in a group of 8 to 15 persons in a room with a rug, devoid of furniture, with all participants sitting on the floor or on pillows. An encounter workshop usually consists of several meetings, each typically 2 hours long, spread over a weekend or over 5 days. Ages vary from 15 to 75 with most participants between 20 and 50. The workshop is held in a residential setting where all participants live. There is no formal agenda. The group focuses on discovering and expressing its feelings in the here-and-now. The group leader helps them to clarify these feelings. All of these conditions for a group are quite variable. The workshop described above is typical of those I will discuss.

There are wide variations in groups called encounter groups and in groups that are called by almost synonymous names, such at T-groups and sensitivity training groups. Even the term encounter is used in different ways by several authors and practitioners. The approach described in this book I have called "open encounter," to distinguish it from the various other encounter groups. Carl Rogers (1970), for example, has used the term basic encounter to name his approach. For simplicity, the term encounter will be used throughout, but it should always be understood to mean open encounter.

3

HISTORY OF ENCOUNTER

Precursors

To look for precursors of the encounter movement is to invite an excursion into speculation and rough equivalents. The Delphic precept, "know thyself," is a succinct statement of a fundamental tenet of encounter. Socrates used group stimulation in his dialogues, although they emphasized intellectual material rather than feelings, a preference not found in encounter.

Perhaps the ancient Greek city of Epidaurus is most closely approximated by a modern growth center such as Esalen in California, a location where, among other activities, encounter group workshops take place. Epidaurus also had its variety of methods concentrating on the body, the unconscious, dreams, and mystical elements. It reputedly had natural hot baths similar to those at Esalen. The Greek legend holds that people were cured of bodily ills by sleeping in the temple of Asclepius, the god of medicine, and having the proper dreams sent to them by the gods. The chief account we have of the activities there comes through the publication, in 1883, of the Epidaurian Temple Record (Herzog, 1931). The importance of this record is stressed by Dodds (1957): "Ever since its publication . . . the gradual change in our general attitude toward nonrational factors in human experience has been reflected in the opinions of scholars."

Insofar as encounter is a form of group therapy, the all-day Greek drama, the medieval morality plays, and Mesmer's large groups of the 1700's are also forerunners. In more modern days, characteristics of encounter groups are found in Quaker meetings in which everyone is silent until someone feels impelled to speak, and in the religious services of the Pentecostals, Holy Rollers, and other such groups in which personal expression through singing and bodily movements is the mode.

4

In an interesting study, Oden (1972) has traced the close connection between modern encounter groups and Western religion, in particular Protestant and Jewish pietism:

The encounter group is a demythologized and secularized form of a style of interpersonal encounter and community which is familiar to historians of Protestant pietism (and also of the Jewish hassidic movement which was parallel to it). Pietism emphasized here-and-now experiencing, intensive small group encounter, honest confession with a trusting community, experimental mysticism, mutual pastoral care, and the operation of the spirit at the level of non-verbal communication.

Hassidic Judaism and Protestant pietism have both been, like current encounter groups, highly syncretistic movements. Wesley's movement, for example, was a practical synthesis of Puritan and Anglican (or more broadly Protestant and Catholic) traditions of faith, practice and communal life (Wesley, 1850). Few of the parts of the synthesis were original with him, but his putting them together in a practical focus, easily implementable in small groups, was a unique and gifted contribution . . . Likewise it is of the essence of the encounter culture today that it is syncretistic, putting together a broad range of change strategies into a working, practical synthesis of resources for human growth in small groups . . .

One thread running through the history of encounter is clearly religious. The assumption that God is within, or works from within you, that you are a vehicle for expressing God, is a common theme. As I gain experience with encounter, it becomes clearer that the encounter goal of realizing one's potential is virtually identical with the religious goal of finding the God within.

Recently Max Lerner, student of American civilization, has traced the history of encounter through the American culture, beginning with Thomas Jefferson and encompassing the Oneida Community, various liberation movements, and several other phenomena (Lerner, 1972b). Lerner sees encounter as the culmination of a variety of indigenous movements that have sprung up in America from its inception to the present.

The encounter assertion of the unity of body and mind has

5

often been alluded to in philosophical and psychological literature. Although some prominent investigators have suggested that the body is the repository of feelings, their lead has not been followed extensively. Sheldon (1949) said over twenty years ago:

> By the unconscious I think psychoanalysts mean the body, however shocking the thought may be to psychoanalysts. The body is really an objectification, a tangible record of the most long-standing and deeply established habits that have been laid down during a long succession of generations. It is the deepest residual and an age-long record of ancestral habit now so firmly established that for the most part it is carried and transmitted in the parental germinal cells.

Gardner Murphy (1971) said:

> We might say, then, that . . . the striped musculature of the arms, hands, trunk, neck, and by implication, other parts of the body, may be conceived to be used all the time in the battle of thought, especially the battle *against* thought . . . most of all, against information unfavorable to the self.

Wilhelm Reich was one of the pioneers of this notion. He wrote (1949):

> The fact that biophysiolocial states are reflected or represented in psychic modes of behavior fits entirely in the framework of our knowledge concerning psychophysical relationships. There is, however, a peculiar fact that is as yet quite obscure: that language as well as the perception of others' behavior renders the respective physiological state unconsciously, not only figuratively, but in an immediate manner. For example: analytic experience shows that if someone is called "inaccessible" and hard he is also muscularly hypertonic. If many patients feels themselves to be "slimy" or "dirty" analysis shows that their character contains largely anal elements.

Reich makes further reference relevant to encounter's insistence on openness and honesty. "If someone is 'false' or 'un-genuine,' analysis shows a prevalence of substitute contacts and an almost complete absence of free-flowing genital libido."

Beginnings

The modern encounter group thus is an integration of a wide variety of influences, ancient and recent. In recent years, various forms of encounter have evolved with amazing rapidity. Since the direction of growth will be seen differently by different leaders in this area, the following account is necessarily idiosyncratic (Schutz 1967, 1971). Many influences have made their mark on the present form of encounter. Below are some:

Group Psychotherapy (Corsini, 1957; Rosenbaum, 1965; Anthony, 1971).

Obviously encounter is closely connected to the development of group psychotherapy, which is usually considered to have started with Pratt in 1907, and which was given great impetus during World War II. Clinical experience revealed that the group had unique properties and was more than a poor substitute for individual therapy.

T-Groups (Bradford *et al.,*1964)

In 1947, several students of psychologist Kurt Lewin organized the first laboratory training centered on T-groups, the "T" standing for "training" (Marrow, 1969). This movement rapidly developed under the leadership of Leland Bradford of the National Training Laboratory. In the early days, NTL emphasized group process and group dynamics. The initial influence of Lewin was supplemented by the psychoanalytically derived formulations of Bion (1961) and the Tavistock school in England. Bion's concepts, expounded in this country primarily by Thelen (1954) and his associates, provided an important theoretical link between the T-group and group psychotherapy (Whitaker and Lieberman, 1964).

In the early 1960's, the West Coast T-group trainers began to have an impact on the direction of NTL. The Western Training Laboratory, begun in 1952 as part of NTL, emphasized individual growth rather than group dynamics (Tannenbaum, *et al.,* 1961). Irving Weschler and Joseph Luft went east to work at NTL's summer workshop in 1961 and 1962 at Bethel, Maine, and there introduced ideas for developing personal growth through the use of the group process. This innovation led to a special advanced workshop at Bethel, in 1963, designed to focus on personal growth and creative expression (Schutz, 1963). The staff of that workshop included Robert Tannenbaum, Charles Seashore, Herbert Shepard, and myself.

The following year, 1964, Californians John and Joyce Weir, led the first Personal Growth laboratory at Bethel. They had a profound effect on NTL by introducing non-verbal techniques into the laboratory design. Typically, they presented their non-verbal methods at a session separate from the T-group meeting. At the same time, I introduced fantasy methods learned from the psychosynthesis group (see below) and began to use some of the Weirs's techniques within the T-group meeting itself.

The Personal Growth laboratory has continued to be a part of the NTL offerings, along with group-oriented and organizational development groups. In 1967, I brought the personal growth form of group, by now called encounter, to the Esalen Institute in Big Sur, California. Over the next few years the encounter group was greatly expanded and modified through incorporation of such techniques as non-verbal communication, psychodrama, fantasy, massage, meditation, yoga, T'ai Chi Ch'uan (a Chinese moving meditation), psychosynthesis (Assagioli, 1965) and gestalt therapy. About this time, Carl Rogers, who had for many years run non-directive counseling groups, became interested in the "intensive group process" and through his prestige attracted great interest to encounter (Rogers, 1970). In 1967, Kairos, the first "growth center" modeled after Esalen, was opened in the San Diego area, and within the next five years no fewer than 200 growth centers had opened in the United States, Canada, Mexico, Holland, Italy, Spain, New Zealand, England, and Israel. Apparently a deep human need was being tapped by the encounter process.

In addition to the hundreds of regular workshops and groups currently offered by growth centers, encounter groups and related activities have sprung up in many churches, social groups, industrial retreats, and universities.

Group Dynamics (Cartwright and Zander, 1953)

In addition to work on the T-group, academicians have given a great deal of attention to research on group phenomena. Many studies have been conducted on group development, phases in group life, leadership, friendship, interpersonal perception, interpersonal attraction, the phenomenon of scapegoating, decision-making, democratic autocratic, and laissez-faire forms of organization, group compatibility, and so on. This area has become one of the most popular in academic social psychology. Many of the concepts, especially theories of group development, which emerged from these investigations, have been central to the growth of encounter (Bion, 1961; Bennis and Shepard, 1956; Schutz, 1966). In a less direct way, academic studies of personality, psychopathology, and learning have been helpful in encounter, particularly as background for the group leader.

Psychodrama (Moreno, 1934)

The techniques developed by Moreno and his colleagues are similar to many used in encounter groups; in fact, some encounter techniques, including role reversal, doubling, and setting up dramatic situations, come directly from psychodrama. Moreno's emphasis on action and non-verbal methods makes his contribution particularly significant. The use of action within the group transports any content into the here-and-now, thereby making it appropriate material for encounter group work.

Gestalt Therapy (Perls *et al.,* 1951)

The technique developed by Frederick Perls is derived from psychodrama and Reich's theories and carries further the intrapsychic emphasis. To help patients understand themselves better, the gestalt technique uses a one-to-one relationship between therapist and patient, in which the therapist uses the patient's here-and-now behavior. This method is used widely within the encounter group setting.

Body Methods

These include rolfing, a method of integrating the body structure through physical repositioning of tense muscles and fascia (Rolf, forthcoming); the exercises of Moshe Felden-krais for freeing the body from its rigid patterns (Feldenkrais, 1972); bioenergetics, a technique derived from Wilhelm Reich combining some psychoanalytic concepts with body work (Lowen), 1967; sensory awareness, a method involving the utmost subtlety in appreciating the nuances of body structure and movement (Selver, 1957); the Alexander technique, based on teaching the body to unlearn unneces-sary movements (Alexander, 1969); hatha yoga (Vish-nudevananda, 1960); and two of the oriental martial arts, Aikido and T'ai Chi Ch'uan, used to understand body balance, centering, and energy (Da Liu, 1972). Each of these procedures has its own history, and the reader is referred to the above publications or to Schutz (1971) where most of them are described briefly.

Theater and Dance

The relationship of encounter to theater and dance is less obvious than its relationship to the above areas, and will be covered at greater length.

On a broad historical basis, there are many resemblances between encounter and theater, such as the encounter "high," that spirit of elation which so often accompanies groups following catharsis, which Greek classical tragedians offered their audiences through the suffering of their lofty heroes. The archaic humor of the Greek "Old Comedy," wit so vulgar, excremental, and nihilistic that it stopped being funny when Athens lost the optimism and high spirits of the Golden Age, may have triggered precisely the same special, curiosly thunderous and therapeutic laughter that often explodes today in the best encounter groups as they move into high gear. Many of the skills of the great dramatists — the dynamics of their choruses, their use of dramatic metaphor, as Oedipus blinded before he can see, have counterparts in encounter groups.

The most towering figure among the modern teacher-directors who developed these theatrical techniques was Constantin Stanislavski (1863-1938) of the Moscow Art Theater.

Stanislavski set about with determination and genius to

find ways of creating good actors in large numbers to staff theatrical companies that would give new life to the Russian stage. His efforts led him into many discoveries about the nature of the theater and of acting. The "sense memory" and "emotional memory" exercises, which he invented and which his American disciple Lee Strasberg has carried on as "the method," have both a practical and a philosophical affinity with encounter and with gestalt therapy, while the animal exercises he encouraged to free actors' inhibitions in the classrooms of the Moscow Art Theater serve much the same purpose in encounter.

Focusing on the actors' abilities to express their inner selves, Stanislavski would repeat to his students, "It is not important that you play well or ill; it is important that you play truthfully" (Stanislavski, 1924). Stanislavski recognized the importance of fantasy life and of the ability to express it. "It was necessary," he wrote "to picture not life itself as it takes place in reality, but as we vaguely feel it in our dreams, our visions, our moments of spiritual uplift." He held that only actors thoroughly grounded in the experience of their own personal truths could reach the heights of artistic force and release, and that this private awareness, perhaps unknowingly, was at the source of the transcendent talents and charismatic presence of all great actors.

Awareness of the widespread use of language as a means of concealment, a point stressed in encounter groups, was stated succinctly for the stage by Julian Beck of the Living Theater, a contemporary American ensemble (Roose-Evans, 1970). "We are not rejecting the use of text in the theater, so much as the use of words to create an alibi," says Beck, and his wife Judith Malina sounds altogether like an encounter group leader as she adds, "If we could once again become feelingful people and not shut ourselves off from one another, then we would not tolerate the injustices of the world. It is part of our process to try to unite mind with body."

Poland's Jerzy Grotowski, one of the major innovators in experimental theater today, expresses an attitude as encounterlike as it is clear (Grotowski, 1963). "If I were to express all this [acting] in one sentence I would say that it is all a question of giving oneself. One must give oneself totally, in one's deepest intimacy, with confidence, as when one gives oneself in love . . . " Viola Spolin (1963), originator of the Improvisational Theater, has written a book describing various theater games, many of which are helpful in encounter groups.

Perhaps the closest relation to the aspect of encounter that encourages doing rather than talking is found in modern dance. "It was Isadora Duncan," writes James Roose-Evans (1970), a young English director, "who first related movement to emotion. Hers was the discovery of the power of movement to evolve its own forms given an emotional impetus . . . It is the essence of modern dance that the movements flow out of ideas, motion from emotion." The religious vision that characterizes recent developments in encounter is also present in modern dance. Martha Graham said, "There is a necessity for movement where words are not adequate. The basis of all dancing is something deep within you. I have always sought to reveal an image of man in his struggle for wholeness, for what you might call God's idea of him, rather than for his own idea of himself." (Roose-Evans, 1970.)

Encounter and the modern theater thus are close cousins, divided only by that thin line where action becomes, to use Aristotle's phrase, the imitation of action. They share specific intentions: to develop the awareness of individuals, to encourage non-verbal communication, to explore inter-personal (actor-spectator) relationships, to deal with nudity, to unite the mind with the body, and to contact the spiritual side, couching this spirit of truth, free of pretentions, in the here-and-now.*

Current Status

Encounter groups are just emerging from a wave of phenomenal growth. From about 1966 to 1971 encounter groups proliferated, and were attacked, defended, publicized, scrutinized, and developed, probably as much as any social science phenomenon in many decades. In 1968, Carl Rogers wrote:

> The Encounter Group is perhaps the most significant social invention of this century. The demand for it is utterly

*My appreciation to Max Furlaud for contributing his expertise in the theater and in literary style to this section.

beyond belief. It is one of the most rapidly growing social phenomena in the United States. It has permeated industry, is coming into education, is reaching families, professionals in the helping fields, and many other individuals.

The great surge of excitement seems now (1972) to be subsiding, and a period of reflection and integration is setting in. Four trends are detectable: (1) The mass of people who have been through encounter groups and liked them want to go on. There is much interest in advanced steps, such as Aikido, psychosynthesis (a total philosophy with techniques of dealing with the whole person including the spirit [Assagioli, 1965]), advanced body techniques, disciplines such as the Arica training (an integrated discipline derived from the Moslem mystical group, the Sufis [Lilly, 1972]), and unorthodox life styles as in communes or unconventional living arrangements. (2) The methods of encounter are being incorporated into the culture. Some psychotherapists are incorporating encounter methods into traditional therapy. In religion, theater, industry, education, and government, encounter methods are being explored and adapted. Evidences of the effects of encounter are seen in more personal contexts, such as family life and parties. Couples' groups are one of the most popular forms of encounter. In such universal reflectors of the culture as cartoons and motion pictures *(Bob and Carol and Ted and Alice; Made for Each Other)*, encounter groups are now fair game. (3) A second wave of interest in encounter is now surfacing in parts of the country that are some distance from the original centers of activity, California and New York. (4) Encounter has become the basis for a life style for many people. In scores of universities the encounter format is being used as a tool for studying a wide variety of courses with such names as human relations, interpersonal communication, group dynamics, and group process. Several observers of the social scene see the influence of encounter on social movements. For example: Confrontation, honesty, demands to "tell it like it is," revolt against the credibility gap, demands for personal liberation and humanistic treatment ("do not fold, spindle, or mutilate me"), emphasis on self-determination of decisions affecting oneself, such as in work or school situations — all reflect principles stressed in encounter. The consideration of a person's own pleasure and desires, the increased acceptance of the body, the religious and spiritual interest, the unity of mind and body, and of self and spirit, also mirror encounter phenomena. In his recent book (1971), Leo Litwak contends that the influence of encounter was central to the rebellion at San Francisco State College.

Training

The most extensive group of people "qualified" to run encounter groups, or more accurately T-groups, is at NTL. Their network of several hundred includes many who have been trained to do T-groups. Few, however, are experienced in the type of groups described here. At Esalen, my colleagues and I have trained about 30 people to be encounter group leaders (see Schutz, 1971, for discussion of training).

Publications

Work in this and related areas is reported in the *Journal of Humanistic Psychology,* the *Journal of Applied Behavioral Science, Group Leader Reports, Interpersonal Development, Group Psychotherapy,* and *Comparative Group Studies.*

Literary Movement

Within the last few years some books have appeared related to the encounter culture. My book, *Joy,* appeared in 1967. Then followed Rasa Gustaitis's *Turning On* (1969) and Jane Howard's *Please Touch* (1970), both surveys of the movement, and John Mann's *Encounter* (1969), Martin Shepard's *Marathon 16* (1970), George Bach's *Intimate Enemy* (1968), Julius Fast's popularized *Body Language* (1971), Alexander Lowen's *Betrayal of the Body* (1967), and George Leonard's *Education and Ecstasy* (1968), which applied the principles to a futuristic view of education. George Brown's *Human Teaching for Human Learning* (1971) reported similar work now taking place in the schools. E. Hunter (1972) also reported on new encounter methods for the classroom. In the academic world, Arthur

Burton edited a book called *Encounter* (1969), and L. Blank and the Gottsegens edited *Confrontation* (1971). Recently Carl Roger's *Carl Rogers on Encounter Groups* (1970) and my *Here Comes Everybody* (1971) have appeared. Viking Press has produced an Esalen series which now numbers 14 books written by various leaders in the field. Fritz Perls's books on gestalt therapy (1951, 1969) have also contributed to this movement, especially his autobiography, *In and Out the Garbage Pail* (1969), which sets a model for encountering one's feelings as one writes. In addition to these current books, there has been an upsurge of interest in writers who have been godfathers to the encounter culture, such as Abraham Maslow (1971), Wilhelm Reich (1949), Georg Groddeck (1949), and Roberto Assagioli (1965).

Encounter is the confluence of many streams of history running from ancient to contemporary times, from different parts of the world, and from diverse fields of interest. These streams seem to have converged in the 1960's in America, and their swift and imaginative integration has led to powerful methods and theories that provide the basis for an important evolutionary step in our relation to ourselves and to one another.

PRINCIPLES OF ENCOUNTER

Unity of the Organism

You are a unified organism. You are at the same time physical, psychological, and spiritual. These levels are all manifestations of the same essence. You function best when these aspects are integrated and when you are self-aware.

Honesty

Honesty and openness are the keys to your evolutionary growth. Being honest allows your bodymind to become a clear channel for taking in all the energy of the universe, both inside and outside your body, and to use it profitably. You must expend great amounts of energy to hide your feelings, thoughts, or wishes from other people, and even more energy to keep them from yourself. To withhold secrets requires a tightened body; it requires curtailment of spontaneity lest the secrets be revealed; it requires vigilance, shallow breathing, physical exertion, and a preoccupation with your own safety. This results in your missing all sorts of stimuli because your bodymind is not relaxed enough to allow them in. The beautiful sights and sounds in nature must not be lingered on too long; the beauty or just the reality of other people cannot be seen clearly because their nuances are too subtle to be caught with rushed glance; the feelings and signals coming from within your own body are strangled by tense muscles, drowned in excess words, or starved from lack of air when you are spending great amounts of energy shaping your appearance in the world.

An issue that may prove important in the future is the effect of dishonesty on other energies in the universe, on the spiritual or mystical energies, which have been hypothesized by millions through the ages and which have become the focus of increasing amounts of serious attention in the last few years. Investigators are beginning to explore stories out of the Middle and Far East of people who, for centuries, have routinely performed feats of transcendence and to explore the recent tales of psychic discoveries in the iron curtain countries (Ostrander and Schroeder, 1971).

If indeed there are other sources of energy available in the universe, for you to avail yourself of these energies probably requires a bodymind sufficiently open to recognize and receive them. "The true, divine self is perfection itself, so a development of it is not possible. Only the body must develop in order to be able to manifest higher and higher vibrations and higher and higher frequencies of the self." (Haich, 1965.) If your body is blocked, tight, and suspicious, it is not likely to be an appropriate receptacle. I believe that honesty and openness, along with the awareness described below, allow for the possibility of tapping the energies usually referred to as spiritual. It is not a guarantee. It seems to be a necessary, though not sufficient, condition. Encounter, therefore, is not the final step in realizing the human potential: it is probably an essential step.

Awareness

A main purpose of encounter is to help you become more aware of yourself: to break through self-deception, to know and like yourself, to feel your own importance, to respect what you are and can do, and to learn to be responsible for yourself. You achieve these best through self-awareness.

Awareness is a life-long process. To live most fully, you must be able to feel all parts of your body, to be able to know what you are feeling at all times, to be aware of your needs and motives no matter how petty or unacceptable, to recognize the personal consequences of your actions, and to integrate all parts of yourself. I believe that an organism in full awareness will choose those actions that are most beneficial for itself, and that a group of organisms functioning together, all in full awareness, will form the most satisfactory society.

Self-deception leads you to manipulative behavior, exploitation, dehumanization, and, ultimately, to unhappiness and lack of productivity. Awareness allows you to make decisions with a maximum of accurate data.

17

Free Choice

Coming to an encounter group is always a voluntary act. Presence in the group assumes that you have chosen to be there. There is no need for concepts such as sick or well, psychotic or normal, neurotic or happy. Choosing to go to an encounter group in no way implies sickness; it implies only a desire for more joy, honesty, self-acceptance, awareness, and so on.

Responsibility

It is important that joining a group be entirely voluntary. If you, as a potential group member, do not feel ready to go to a group, or if you have a dread of being brainwashed, denuded, robbed of all privacy, made dependent, or of any of the other horrors vividly described by Koch (1971), Argyris (1966), and others, your path is clear: Don't go. As the group leader, I routinely announce that you are responsible for making the choice of entering the encounter group, and that you are responsible for everything that happens to you during the life of the group. All choices about yourself are yours. You may choose to have your brain washed or to use your judgment, to go crazy or to be sane, to learn something or to be inert, to be bored or to be interested, to enjoy or to be miserable, to resist or welcome efforts at opening you up, to reveal your sexual intimacies or to keep them secret, to be physically injured or remain intact. I regard you as capable of being responsible for yourself.

By assuming that you are responsible, I feel I elicit your stronger parts. If I assume that you are not capable of being responsible, I tend to infantilize you and elicit your weaker parts. The medical model, "I am the doctor, and I have the knowledge and ability to cure you, and you are the patient who is sick and requires my help," I see as usually debilitating.

My assertion that you are self-responsible does not mean that I cannot choose to be responsible for you. I decide how responsible for you I want to make myself. This attitude often leads to more initial anguish on your part and also to more important growth, than does one that is more nurturing. Henry Miller recognized the importance of self-responsibility in his own unique way (1972):

> In Paris about 1934 I died. I mean spiritually, I took
> everything on my shoulders. I decided I was responsible. I
> didn't blame my parents, my background, society, school
> — I was the one responsible. And what a relief it was, that
> day in Paris when I had a vision of how things were. I
> really saw myself clearly for the first time. I said I can no
> longer blame anybody. From now on, I take the respon-
> sibility. Instead of being a burden I threw everything off.
> No more guilt, no regrets, nobody to blame, nobody
> blames nobody. You have to accept yourself. There you
> are for what you are. There are no perfect beings. Once
> you get that idea you throw off a lot again.

Naturalness

I trust natural processes. My reliance on natural unfolding
extends to virtually every facet of human functioning.
Encounter involves removing psychological blocks so that
you may flow freely and naturally. Body methods aim at
removing physical blocks so that your energy may flow
freely. Confidence in the natural flow of human energy
extends to many areas of experience. The ideal diet is one
that your aware body selects as its way of maintaining health;
the preferred forms of medicine are those which remove
obstacles to your body's processes for healing itself; the
preferred group situation is one that lets you unfold.

Way of Life

Encounter is a way of life, not just a therapeutic
technique. It concerns itself with relations among people and
offers an alternative to the present structure of society, a
structure which is based on deception ("diplomacy"), mask-
ing feelings ("tact"), disowning the body ("primitive, irrational, obscene"), and similar duplicities.

The encounter culture follows the counter culture. It puts
flesh on the bones of "Consciousness III" (Reich, 1971). It
provides a way for human beings to relate to each other that
is different from the devious way now dominant. It arises
from the inner revolution that is changing the nature of
individuals.

Openness and honesty are at the heart of the encounter culture. This means not lying to others and also means avoiding self-deception. The encounter culture appreciates and emphasizes feelings as well as thoughts. It recognizes the central place of feelings in the internal and interpersonal aspects of people and devises means for recognizing and dealing effectively with them. It recognizes the centrality of the body in human affairs, the truth that resides there, and the body's role as the repository of a person's history and as the source of a person's pleasure. The encounter culture accepts the unity of body, mind, and spirit and the importance of working at all levels simultaneously. It recognizes the importance of naturalness and reality, of going back to the natural organism, and of knowing and accepting the reality of what a person is without overburdening a person with "shoulds."

The encounter culture stresses individual responsibility. You are responsible for whatever you are; therefore, you can change. You are not a victim of forces far greater than yourself. The encounter culture focuses on enjoying the here-and-now. While not excluding pleasant memories or exciting anticipations, it recognizes that the now is all that is ever experienced. The encounter culture holds that all pleasures reside in the now.

In what sense is all this a culture? These principles, in part or as a whole, are sweeping over large areas of this country at a rapid rate. The responsible journalist Max Lerner has suggested an encounter group for the President and for all presidential candidates (Lerner, 1972a). While there has not yet occurred a coalescence of these areas into any single institution, such as a political party or a university, the sheer breadth, diversity, and rate of growth of these ideas indicates that coalescence may not be long in coming.

Other Systems

Encounter differs from most other group methods in that it stresses body methods, non-verbal techniques, and guided daydream fantasies. It also emphasizes self-responsibility and expands the meaning of that term to include responsibility for the state of the body. Unlike most other systems of directed change, it does not require M.D.'s or Ph.D.'s as leaders (the complex qualifications for encounter group leadership are discussed in Schutz, 1971). Encounter is also unusual in its attempts to integrate methods from a particularly wide variety of approaches. Like John Wesley, it is "syncretistic." Since experience happens to the whole body, encounter assumes that the experience can be understood and responded to faster by involving the whole person.

The major reason for incorporating a large variety of methods into encounter is that nothing works for everyone. It seems more valuable to determine the conditions under which each method works most effectively than to determine which among various methods is the "best." The idea that people are different from one another, although one of the least controversial ideas in psychology, is rarely thoroughly understood. There are persons whose lives are dramatically changed through a weekend encounter and some who are relatively unaffected by several groups. The same may be said of persons who undergo psychoanalysis, psychodrama, behavior therapy, gestalt, fantasy, rolfing, or virtually any other method. The challenge is to find out for which people, at what points in their personal development, and with which leader each method or pattern of methods works best. As an encounter group leader, my aim is to become proficient in as many techniques as I find useful and, through experience, to learn when to use which.

PHYSIOLOGICAL BASIS OF ENCOUNTER

For clarity of presentation, I shall use "I" to represent the universal self when describing the physiological and psychological bases of encounter.

My body is born with an inherent potential for growth. Under optimal conditions all my organs will grow to their capacity in size, strength, function, and flexibility. Part of this growth — vegetative functions, emergency reactions, and so on — is coordinated by the lower centers of the brain, is primarily inherited, and only with great difficulty, or by esoteric methods (such as biofeedback, Barber, *et al.,* 1971), is subject to alteration by external conditions. The cortex, the higher brain center, controls another part of the growth of my body; this part is subject to external conditions, among them learning. I differ from lower animals in that a relatively small percentage of my capacity is instinctive and in that a relatively large proportion is subject to learning (Feldenkrais, 1972).

As I develop, if my tissues and organs are all used in the various ways in which they are capable of being used, I will realize my full potential. Of course, I won't. No one does. Three factors prevent it: physical trauma, emotional trauma, and limited use.

To see how these factors inhibit growth, conceive of me as a process rather than as a static entity (Keleman, 1971). Most of my body is, in fact, in constant change. Except for the nervous system, all my body cells are replaced approximately every two to seven years. I may be viewed as a process through time, starting at the moment the sperm enters the ovum.

As my body/person/process evolves through time, my optimal unfolding is influenced by the three factors mentioned above. The distinction between natural, or unimpeded, evolution and optimal evolution is important.

Unimpeded development, that is, development without trauma, will not lead my body to develop to its full potential. Lack of interference with my sense of sound during childhood will not assure me a concertmaster's ear. My ear will be unflawed, but not extraordinary. Similarly, growing up without being impeded does not guarantee full growth of personality, as shown by classic studies of babies raised without sufficient handling (Spitz, 1945; Goldfarb, 1943).

As my body/person/process evolves through time, trauma and limited use begin to affect the form of my body, just as strong winds, fires, overcrowding, and periodic lack of nourishment affect the growth of a tree. As with the tree, the effect of these external influences may be read by observing my physical structure.

Physical Trauma

Physical trauma can interfere with my natural growth process (Rolf, forthcoming), just as pruning reduces a full grown tree to a midget bonsai. Suppose I break an ankle early in life. During the healing process, I feel unsteady on my feet and throw my weight forward onto my toes. If I do not compensate for this imbalance, I will fall forward. I may compensate by tightening the muscles in the small of my back. If these muscles become too strong, I will fall backward; thus, I must make another compensation by thrusting my head forward. When I balance my body in this way, the muscles in my legs, back, and neck feel tense.

If I adopt this posture, eventually the muscle tensions become chronic, and my connective tissue grows to hold these muscles in a rigid position. My muscles lose their ability to flex and relax appropriately. Related structures are affected. My tight muscles, for example, may constrict a local blood vessel, partially closing it, and may restrict the blood supply to neighboring areas; or my lungs may be prevented from inflating fully, thus cutting down on the oxygen supply; or the spinal nerves issuing from my aberrated spine may be impinged upon and nerve impulses to the corresponding organs impaired. These difficulties may heighten my susceptibility to disease of the affected organ. The impingement of nerves through misalignment of vertebrae (subluxations) is

23

the subject matter of the field of chiropractic (Gallert, 1966).

Poor nutrition, as well as physical trauma, affects my body chemistry and can have a deleterious affect on my development. It can affect mental functioning, energy level, and personality.

Emotional Trauma

Emotional trauma can also alter the course of physical development as has been shown especially by work in psychosomatics (Simeons, 1961) and bioenergetics (Reich, 1949; Lowen, 1958). The flow of my body/person/process is impeded by emotional trauma. Whenever I have a feeling I want to express, and a conflicting feeling inhibits its expression, I am left with a tension in my body. This is particularly true if I am not aware of the conflict. If the same out-of-awareness conflict occurs frequently, my tense muscle will become chronic. Suppose that when I was a child, I was never allowed to express my anger. When I got angry, I wanted to bite, my eyes narrowed, my fists clenched, my shoulders drew back, my stomach tightened to prepare to strike, my stance widened to prepare for a counter-blow. But my parents forbade the completion of these incipient actions. Soon my parents' prohibitions were internalized, and whenever I felt anger I inhibited myself. If this inhibition occurred frequently, very likely my jaw muscles would be chronically tense, my eyes would form a permanent narrowing, my forearms would be chronically tight, my shoulders would be held back, my stomach muscles would be very tense, and my stance would be a permanent straddle. The interdependence of my body organs is such that my digestion, excretion, breathing, and so on, are affected by these changes in my body. Certain illnesses, such as stomach trouble, now become more probable because my body tensions weaken organs, making them more vulnerable to disease.

More obviously, emotional traumas affect emotional development. Not only is my physical organism altered, but also my emotionality is affected in the areas relevant to the trauma. If, for example, a childhood trauma resulted in fear of my mother and left a conflicted tendency to run away from her, then it is likely that my feeling toward women who

24

remind me of my mother will be processed through that "run away" muscle tension. My reaction to them will be contaminated. This is the phemonenon known as transference.

Limited Use

The third obstacle to my optimal unfolding is not as pathological as emotional trauma. It may arise from social or psychological origins, from lack of knowledge, or from physical causes. Although my body parts are capable of moving in countless combinations, as I grew up only a very small proportion of these combinations were used.

This restriction is easily demonstrated. As you read this, stop and turn your head to the right . . . It is probable that you also turned your eyes to the right, although the instruction did not require or even suggest it. Independent movement of the head and eyes is rarely required. We are so accustomed to moving them together that the possibility of differentiated movement does not even occur to us.

Try folding your hands. Now fold them the other way: if your right index finger was above your left index finger, reverse them, putting your left on top . . . Probably, you experience the second as quite strange, off-balance, and perhaps even uncomfortable, almost as if there were a right and a wrong way to fold your hands. This is, of course, absurd, but our habitual patterns so limit our movements that we become alienated from many movement possibilities in our own bodies. Physical limitations also reflect emotional, sensational, and intellectual limits (Feldenkrais, 1972).

That the bodymind is capable of far more than most of us use is amply demonstrated by specialists. Specific movements or patterns of movements are developed to a high degree by certain professionals. Acrobats can move their pelvic muscles through a wide range of motion far beyond the ability of the average person; yogis have control of their breathing; chess masters have developed their analytical ability; weight lifters, their strength; piano tuners, their ability to discriminate sounds. All have developed in ways that many average people might have developed, but have not. Certain occupations require the rapid integration of a large number of activities. A football quarterback, for instance, within a few seconds must feel the football, turn it to the proper position for throwing, place his hand on it to throw, look for one or more receivers, step behind his blockers, move to avoid onrushing tacklers, fake a pass to one side of the field, look to the other, judge how hard and where to throw, and decide whether to throw or run. Thus he must coordinate sight, sound, judgment, movement, and effort, and he must do it all at once.

When I use a set of muscles in only one movement pattern, I have difficulty using other patterns with ease. An obvious example is the learning of a language. During this process, the muscles of my mouth, tongue, vocal cords, neck, and breathing apparatus are trained in certain ways in order to make the appropriate sounds. My muscles accommodate to these positions with the result that certain sounds in another language are difficult for me to make since my musculature has been set. If my native tongue is English, this difficulty is especially evident when I try to pronounce German guttural or French nasal sounds. Achieving the freedom to use alternate combinations of muscles requires me to overcome built-in resistances.

Lowen (1970) has stressed the intimate relationships between movement and other activities:

The functional identity of thinking and feeling stems from their common origin in body movement. Every movement of the body that is perceived by the conscious mind gives rise to both a feeling and a thought. The concept that body movements give rise to feelings and thoughts run counter to ordinary thinking . . . Seen from below, movement not only precedes but also provides the substance for our feelings and thoughts. We are accustomed to see movement as a result of thinking and feeling rather than the other way around. These informative movements are the involuntary bodily movements. Volitional movements, on the other hand, proceed from feeling and thought.

Lowen also make the point, similar to Feldenkrais's, that movement is central to human functioning: "If thinking stems from movement, it follows that man's greater thinking capacity derives ultimately from the greater range of movements that he is capable of performing." (Lowen, 1970.)

In a series of ingenious exercises, Feldenkrais (1972)

demonstrates how physical limitations can be overcome. He feels that by practicing unusual movements we can send new messages to the nervous system, which allows it, in turn, to send new messages to the muscles. This process releases some of the built-in restrictions and allows the body more freedom and mobility. In addition to the increased freedom of movement, functions controlled by the nervous system are also freed, including feeling, thinking, and sensing. Here, condensed, is an example of Feldenkrais exercise:

Feldenkrais Exercise

Stand with your right arm extended straight out in front of you at shoulder level. Look at your hand and turn your arm, head, and eyes together to the right as far as they will go without strain. Note a point on the wall corresponding to that distance. Now swing back slowly to the front position. Let your arm down and relax . . . Raise it again to the front position. Move your arm to the right as before, but at the same time move your head to the left. Move both head and arm as far as you can without strain. Do this five times, returning to the center position between trials. Be aware of the feelings in your neck, shoulders and waist during these five movements. Put your arm down and relax . . . Now once again try the original motion of raising your arm, looking at your hand, and moving your arm, head, and eyes to the right as far as they will go without strain. Compare it with the original point on the wall. You will probably observe that you move considerably farther. Put your arm down and relax . . . Again put your arm in the front position. Now move your arm to the right and your head and hips (pelvis) to the left, all as far as they will go without strain. Do this five times, returning to the center position between trials. Be very aware of all your body movements. Put your arm down and relax . . . Again try the original movement, moving your arm to the right as far as you can go without strain. Compare the distance your arm now travels with the original distance. It is probable that your arm again turns noticeably farther to the right than it did before. Come back to the center, put your arm down and relax.

Now hold your left arm straight out in front, look at your

left hand and turn your head, trunk, and arm to the left as far as you can without strain and note the point on the wall. Come back to the front. Put your arm down. Relax . . . Put it up again in the front position. Now, *only in your imagination,* repeat the first movements made with the right arm three times each. That is, imagine your left arm going left and your head going right, three times. Then imagine your arm going left and your head and hips going right three times. While you do this, concentrate on the muscle feelings. Try to see three clear movements. After the imagined movement, open your eyes, put your arm down, and relax . . . Now put your left arm in front as before, look at your hand, and move your arm, trunk, and head to the left and note the difference in the point on the wall. There will probably be almost as large an increment as with the right side, although it was gained without any movement.

Recent work on the involuntary nervous system provides an explanation for the ideational part of this exercise and for the bodymind view generally. Miller (1969) says:

> Cellular electric current can be made to occur in protoplasm by the very act of thinking. Thought alone can therefore, in and of itself, be the stimulus to induce an electric current to flow down any nerve to the affected tissue — demonstrating that thought is a source of energy. . . . the Involuntary Nervous System is not necessarily involuntary . . . it is more under our conscious control than previously believed.

Expression of Emotions

In a comprehensive review and integration of research on emotions, Izard (1971) emphasizes these conclusions:

1. The organism is unified as expressed by the interdependence of various levels of functioning.

2. The body is central in understanding emotions. Motor activity is crucial to the expression of feelings.

3. Natural feelings expressed through motor action are suppressed by cultural factors.

Each of these conclusions has important implications for the theory of human growth as related to encounter.

Unity of the Organism

Since an emotion exists simultaneously at many levels of the organism, its alteration can best be accomplished by altering all levels. Changes in one level affect the other levels; a strategy to effect growth, therefore, is to find the most accessible level and work there, or better, to work at several levels at once.

Izard defines emotion in this way:

Emotion is a complex concept with neurophysiological, neuromuscular and phenomenological aspects. At the neurophysiological level emotion is defined primarily in terms of patterns of electrochemical activity in the nervous system . . . At the neuromuscular level emotion is primarily facial patterning, and secondarily it is body (postural-gestural, visceral and sometimes vocal) response. At the phenomenological level emotion is essentially motivating experience and/or experience which has immediate meaning and significance for the person. I make the assumption that the experiencing of emotion can constitute a process in consciousness, completely independent of cognition.

The experimental results thus support the encounter practice of dealing with the facial, body, and conscious levels directly, as aspects of the same experience.

Motor Aspects

Izard (1971) summarizes the work of Darwin (1872), William James (1884), F.H. Allport (1924), Cannon (1929), Jacobson (1929), Gellhorn (1970), Pesso (1969), Plutchik (1962), and Tomkins (1962) — concluding that emotion involves centrally the striate ("voluntary") musculature. Perhaps the best statement of this position comes from Gellhorn: "Emotional behavior can be controlled via the somatic system; or, to express it differently, that emotions can be controlled by willed action of the musculature." (Gellhorn, 1970.)

In encounter, attention to the muscular system is central. By holding muscles under tension, a person suppresses feelings. This gives rise to an important rule of encounter: "Whenever there is an opportunity to express something physically, rather than verbally, do it physically." If, for example, you would like to make contact with another person, it is preferable for you to move over and touch that person rather than simply to keep talking. Staying immobile except for verbalizing is a way to suppress the feeling, as is pointed out above, in the second principle derived by Izard.

Suppression

Izard states that infants express emotions spontaneously with the muscles of their faces and bodies and that by about the end of the first year their facial musculature is sufficiently well developed to express all common emotions:

> In early childhood then there is a mutually reinforcing relationship between maturing facial musculature and evolving emotions. But as socialization and other emotion control practices suppress the display of externally observable facial patterns of emotion, cognitive development makes possible the substitution of a symbol (memory or image) for the actual motor pattern. The memory image may be reinforced or supplemented by slight and micro-momentary facial movement. The diminished facial activity and the symbol substitution mechanism may become devices capable to some extent of regulating and controlling the emotions. (Izard, 1971).

This statement supports the emphasis given by group leaders to helping members become aware of their facial and postural gestures, and the relative inattention they give to the words (images) used to describe emotions. Body manifestations are closer to spontaneous feeling, while words are closer to expressing the cultural overlays, though, of course, they frequently coincide. Often the external image offered to the world is expressed by an automatic facial expression, such as a constant smile. If a person drops the automatic expression, the person may contact the real feeling, sadness perhaps, that it hides.

The fascinating notion of the micromomentary expression, described by Haggard and Isaacs (1966), is illuminating. While scanning motion pictures of psychotherapy interviews, these investigators found: "Occasionally the expression on a client's face would change dramatically within three to five frames of film (as from smile to grimace to smile), the equivalent of 1/8 to 1/5 of a second." The changes were so rapid that they were not detectable at the normal speed of the film. Investigation of these micromomentary expressions showed that they were directly related to the psycho-dynamics of the relation between patient and the person the patient was discussing at the time.

In encounter, momentary expressions, along with similar body movements, are a focus of the leader's attention and eventually of the attention of the group members. Since they represent strongly suppressed impulses, the person exhibiting them is asked to repeat and exaggerate them. This enlarge-ment compensates for the diminishing of the original impulse through cultural or other suppression. The exaggeration of a momentary expression thus brings the feeling closer to its original intensity.

An example of this phenomenon occurred recently in an academic group when an administrator was asked a difficult question. He flicked a piece of dirt off his trousers and began in measured tones to respond. The verbal response repre-sented his second feeling, the culturally acceptable response. The first, spontaneous feeling was revealed by the flicking finger. If I had focused on the words, much time would have been lost in a verbal maze justifying and covering up the first, still unknown, feeling. I asked the administrator to stop talking and to flick the dirt off his trousers over and over, allowing the gesture to grow stronger and stronger, and accompanying it with any sounds that came out of his throat, until he got in touch with a feeling. When his true feelings surfaced, they were anger and a desire to dismiss his questioner with a flick of the finger.

If you, as a group member, are talking and do not seem to be getting anywhere, I, as the leader, may ask you to start moving your muscles, thus helping you to be in touch on a more active level with the feeling that your words are hiding. If two of you are trying to express how you feel about each other verbally and are not making progress, I may ask you to sit in front of each other and communicate without words. This often results in hugging, wrestling, pushing away, turning around, or in the emergence of some concealed desire, once the verbal overlay is removed.

This does not mean that verbalizing is never of value. After you become aware of a feeling, a verbal exploration of it is often solidifying and illuminating. When verbalizing masks the underlying feeling, however, it is best to stop the talk and explore body feelings.

These findings question all *strictly* verbal therapies. Since an essential part of every emotion is its physical expression, the therapist who allows you, the patient, to sit (or lie) immobile, perhaps not even moving your face, probably can elicit only a limited portion of your feelings. It follows that such therapies would take far longer for success than those that involve the body. Failure to recognize the economy of using the body is a reason that encounter is often accused of being too quick and, therefore, superficial ("instant joy," "instant cure" [Perls, 1967]). Since the time necessary to bring out real feelings can be greatly reduced through use of movement and gesture, progress is typically more rapid than in traditional therapies; this may give the false impression that such progress is superficial.

Energy Cycles

Throughout the theoretical and practical development of encounter, one concept recurs constantly: energy. Energy not only determines what happens within my person/body/process, it is also one of the main elements with which I, as an encounter group leader, work. My effectiveness depends, in large part, on my ability to detect and use group and individual energy.

The difference between a living and a dead organism is the presence or absence of energy manifestations. The size, weight, and chemical constituents of a living body and one newly dead are virtually the same, but from the latter the energy is gone. Body energies include flow of nerve currents, contraction of muscles, circulation of blood, generation of heat, movement of food through the alimentary system, movement of air through the respiratory system, and repair of cellular structures. There are also group energies and perhaps cosmic or spiritual energies, which are more difficult to measure. Many illnesses can be seen as a disturbance of the energy process.

An energy cycle has four phases: motivation, preparation, performance, and consummation (note similarity to those described by George Herbert Mead in *The Philosophy of the Act* [1938]). When I have a need, my energy is mobilized in the muscles, which prepare for discharge. If my energy is not spontaneously and appropriately released, it may seep out in such small, unsatisfying movements as the jiggling of a foot, the clenching of a jaw, or the furrowing of a brow. If, however, there is no discharge at all, the energy may manifest itself as nervousness, muscle tension, dizziness, headache, or weariness (Schutz, 1971).

A good example of an energy cycle is the running of a race. As an athlete, I go from a relaxed state before I start thinking about the race, to a state of preparation just before it. My preparation is often accompanied by running up and down, talking nervously, setting my jaw, jiggling, and by butterflies in my stomach and sweat on my palms. My anxiety increases on the starting line, often resulting in false starts, that is, non-productive discharges of energy. The preparations my body has made come to fruition as the race begins, and my muscles go into action until the race is finished. Usually, after the race, I have a need to consolidate the experience. My breath returns and sometimes I need to vomit in order to discharge the remaining energy. Finally, I return to my original state, perhaps depressed if I lost, often euphoric if I did well, and feeling good for the exertion. If I don't complete the race, I don't feel relaxed. These phases of an energy cycle are recognized by the familiar manner in which numerous events are started: on your mark — get set — go. This almost states: get yourself motivated — prepare your body — perform. The outcome of the activity corresponds to the consummation of the energy cycle.

Kurt Lewin's notion of tension systems that lead to action until the tension is released is similar to the idea of the energy cycle. Lewin's relative inattention to the body, however, may have prevented him from taking a further step. In contrasting historic (primarily psychoanalytic) and systematic (field theory) explanations, Lewin said:

If only the present state of the person influences his behavior today, as topological psychology claims, and if at the same time certain experiences and structures of the child have a direct influence on the adult, as psycho-analysis claims, one would have to assume an immense rigidity of acquired structures within a living being. (See Marrow, 1969.)

Lewin also noted that the extent to which the dynamic structure of the person remains unchanged during develop-ment and the way in which changes do occur constitute "one of the basic problems of psychology" (Marrow, 1969). More recent body work, especially rolfing (Rolf, forthcoming) and bioenergetics (Lowen, 1967), indicates that the body does indeed have many rigid structures, or blocks, and also many elastic parts. Both the rigidities and flows can be detected in the physical structure.

Body Interpretation

My entire history is in my body. The aspects of myself that were well developed and unimpeded emerge as well-functioning, developed body parts: strong, flexible muscles, clear, well-seeing eyes, efficient blood circulation, and so on. The parts of my body that are undernourished reflect neglect at some point in my life. Muscles tensions, decrements in physiological functioning, and imbalances in movement and physical structure reflect blockages, limitations, and traumas. The earlier and more significant the trauma, the deeper it is found in my body structure.

Identification of the psychological meaning of the various physical aberrations will be discussed below. One main principle, however, will be advanced here: If, in my past, I have repeatedly experienced a traumatic feeling, my body appears as if it were presently experiencing that feeling. For example, if childhood was sad and lonely, I probably have the look of someone who is sad and lonely: dark, sad, deep-set eyes, turned down mouth, sagging shoulders, weak legs. If high achievement was always expected of me, I probably have the look of someone who is always vigilant so as not to miss anything and who is anxious about being tested. I may frown a lot and may have a vertical line between my eyebrows, exceptionally good vision (vigilance), tight neck muscles to help me not to "lose my head," shallow breathing to be always ready, and so forth.

If my body functioning is limited, in the Feldenkrais sense, I may have become that way through social pressure or through lack of an imaginative and challenging environment. Social pressure can lead, for example, to what Reich (1949) calls character armor, a pattern of muscle tensions used to cope with the world. One example is the frozen pelvis. Because social taboos prohibit moving the pelvic area either forward and backward or sideways (bump and grind), the flesh around my pelvis builds up and sits without movement. My hips and upper legs become large in proportion to the rest of my body. I have a buildup of fatty tissue, which, due to diminished blood flow, is whiter and cooler than the surrounding tissue.

An unimaginative environment induces limits by accepting only one pattern of movement for performing an act. An assembly line worker who uses the same motion constantly, a dancer of fixed-pattern dances, and a marching military man are examples of regimented and limiting body movement. Young children, playing spontaneously, move in a wide variety of ways. The imposition of adult values soon reduces this variety.

A typical school is a good example. An important characteristic of a "good" classroom is the relative immobility of the children — sitting quietly at desks, perhaps with hands folded. An immobile child rarely gets in trouble. It is the active one moving in unconventional, therefore unacceptable ways, that gets into difficulty. These experiences later appear as limitations of movement and of coordination throughout the child's body. It tends to be stiff and ungraceful.

Physiological work on the nervous system provides a scientific basis for these observations. Recent theorizing (Simeons, 1961; Feldenkrais, 1972) distinguishes at least two parts of the brain. Simeons speaks of the cortex and diencephalon; Feldenkrais speaks of the superlimbic, the limbic, and the rhinic parts. In each case, the parts referred to are evolutionarily different. The lower, rhinic (diencephalon) system is earlier in evolution and physically lower, while the upper part (cortex) is of more recent development and physically higher in the body. The lower system is primarily instinctive; the upper, more conscious, thinking.

The lower system, according to these theorists, acts instantly in the presence of threat, often before the upper nervous system is aware of the situation. When I slip on a banana peel, before I am fully aware of what has happened, my body has made immediate adjustments to right the balance and preserve my upright posture. My brain does not give the conscious directions: "Now, put your left foot back, bend your head forward," and so forth. These movements are done automatically through my lower brain centers.

Having this lower nervous system available is, of course, of enormous survival value, but it can also be the source of great difficulty when it is not understood. Simeons believes the lack of proper interpretation of the lower nervous system to be the source of psychosomatic ailments. Suppose, for example, that my family has a history of heart trouble and that I am in a situation that is psychologically threatening. Unaware of my fear, I try to appear calm. I become aware, however, of my rapidly beating heart, a physiological change brought about by the lower system to prepare my body to cope with threat. Because I am unaware of my anxiety, the true source of the accelerated heart beat, I misinterpret my body's signal to be an indication of a weak heart.

The alarm or stress reaction affects my adrenals, which leads to an increase in the supply of blood to the muscles. The muscles increase their tone and hold a slight tension that permits quicker action. If I am in this state of tension, body massage is of little value because my lower nervous system is sending continuous signals to the muscles to remain tense. I can relax only by communicating to the lower nervous system that the danger has passed. I can do this either directly through my body, or by providing awareness to the cortex that I am anxious and having the cortex notify the lower system. The psychological aim is for the upper brain center to understand and control the lower centers except in those cases in which the automatic response of the lower is more efficient.

Summary

My person/body/process begins as sperm penetrates ovum. Three blockages prevent normal development: physical trauma, emotional trauma, and limited use. My body develops to the degree that I use it, to the degree that it completes energy cycles. To be fully realized, I must complete many of these energy cycles repeatedly. The three blockages slow my energy flow and build blocks into my physical structure. These blocks diminish my physiological functioning, leading to reduced blood supply, less oxygen, impeded nervous impulses, reduced organ funtion, diminished intellectual capacity, and, eventually, to physical and emotional illness.

Further, these blocks influence my body's physical structure and function, including my facial expression, posture, growth, flexibility of movement, skin tone, and distribution of fat. With practice, you can read my personal history from the structure of my body. If I am unaware of what is happening in my body, I may become both physically and mentally ill. My lack of awareness manifests itself psychologically as self-deception. In its aim, the realization of the human potential, encounter is close to the esoteric psychological schools and to the ancient and modern mystical religions that seek the knowledge of the Higher, Immortal Self, the Krishna-consciousness, or Christ-consciousness, which can guide the self's evolutionary growth toward the Self. Concepts of what is "normal," "right," or of what "should be" are obstructions to seeing what is. As Metzner puts it (1971): " 'For the kingdom of heaven is within you,' and the goal of the path of evolutionary growth and development, according to the most ancient and sacred teachings, is to learn to follow the inner direction of the Higher Self, so that we can externalize the divinity within, and it will 'be on earth as it is in heaven.' "

PSYCHOLOGICAL BASIS OF ENCOUNTER

The key psychological notion in encounter theory is the self-concept. My self-concept is largely derived from my relations with other people. In my dealings, I exchange various "commodities" with people and make adjustments. In order to understand this interpersonal level of functioning, I shall use the framework introduced in the book *FIRO* (Schutz, 1966).

I have three basic interpersonal needs. They are manifested in behavior and feelings toward other people and are rooted in my feelings about myself, my self-concept. The three need areas are posited to be *inclusion, control,* and *affection.*

Inclusion refers to my feelings about being important, significant or worthwhile. Control refers to my feelings of competence, including intelligence, appearance, practicality, and ability to cope with the world. Affection revolves around my feelings of being lovable, of feeling that if my personal essence is revealed in its entirety, it will be seen as a lovely thing.

Inclusion

Inclusion behavior refers to associations between people, exclusion, inclusion, belonging, togetherness. The need to be included manifests itself as wanting attention and interaction. Revolutionaries are often objecting mostly to the lack of attention paid them. Even negative attention partially satisfies them.

An integral part of inclusion is that I am uniquely distinguishable from other people. To be fully identifiable is to be understood, since it implies that someone is interested enough in me to discover my unique characteristics.

The issue of commitment arises frequently at the outset of group relations. In the initial testing of a relationship, I usually present myself to others partly to find out what facet

38

of myself will interest them. Sometimes, however, I am silent because I am not sure that others care about what I have to say.

Unlike the affection area, inclusion does not involve my strong emotional attachments to other individuals. It differs from control in that my preoccupation is with prominence rather than with dominance. Since inclusion involves the process of group formation, it usually occurs as the earliest interpersonal issue in the life of a group. I first decide whether I want to be part of the group.

If I am an *undersocial,* a person who has too little inclusion, I tend to be introverted and withdrawn. I consciously want to maintain distance between myself and others and insist that I do not want to get enmeshed with others and lose my privacy. Unconsciously, however, I definitely want others to pay attention to me. My greatest fear is that people will ignore me and will prefer to leave me behind. My unconscious attitude may be summarized: "Since no one is interested in me, I'm not going to risk being ignored. I'll stay away from people and get along by myself." I have a strong drive toward self-sufficiency as a technique for existence without others. Behind my withdrawal is the private feeling that others do not understand me. My deepest anxiety is that I am worthless. Unconsciously, I feel that since no one ever considered me important enough to receive attention, I must be of no value whatsoever.

If I am an *oversocial* person, I tend toward extroversion. I seek people incessantly and want them to seek me out. I am also afraid that they will ignore me. My unconscious feelings are the same as those of the withdrawn person, but my overt behavior is the opposite. My unconscious attitude may be summarized: "Although no one is interested in me, I'll make people pay attention to me in any way I can. I always seek companionship, for I cannot stand to be alone."

My interpersonal behavior is designed to focus attention on myself, to make other people notice me, to be prominent. My direct method is to be an intense, exhibitionistic participant. By simply forcing myself on the group, I force the group to focus their attention on me. My subtle technique for gaining attention is to seek to be powerful (control) or well-liked (affection). My inclusion problems often lead me to vacillate between oversocial and undersocial behavior.

If I am a *social,* a person whose problem of inclusion was successfully resolved in childhood, my interaction with people presents no problem. I am comfortable with or without others. I can be a high or low participant in a group, without feeling anxious. I am capable of strong commitment to and involvement with certain groups, but I can also withhold commitment if I feel it is appropriate to do so. Unconsciously, I feel that I am a worthwile, signficant person.

On the physical level, inclusion is related to the boundaries between myself and the rest of the world, and therefore deals primarily with the periphery of my body, the skin and sense organs, eyes, ears, nose, and mouth. Attitudes toward these organs may be related to my attitudes toward being included by others.

If I fear contact with others, my eyes keep other people from intruding by not seeing them clearly. In order to see others clearly, I put up a barrier, glasses. When I look at something that I do not really want to see, my eyes become dull and seem to retire to the back of my head (Kelley, 1972). When I do not want inclusion, my ears hear people who are close as if they were far away. Not wanting to be close, I keep other people at a distance. My mouth and lips become tight and impenetrable. My skin shies away from being touched and is easily tickled. I get pimples, rashes, and hives easily so that people will not come near. The muscles of my skin may also tighten so that my sensitivity is minimized. My skin feels leathery to the touch.

If being included is important to me, my body may reflect it by having these peripheral organs perform in the opposite way. My senses of smell and hearing are acute, bringing far things near. My skin is receptive to touch and is open and soft. My eyes are vigilant, looking for people in order to see them clearly. I try to see people who are far away as actually being closer. This effort may lead to especially good vision and, perhaps, to vertical lines between my eyebrows. I realize that I have voluntary control of my vision when I look at you in two ways. First, I look at you dully, as if my eyes were open but actually located way back in my head. I see as little as possible while appearing to give you attention. When I imagine my eyes leaping out and grabbing you, however, I feel in much closer contact with you.

Various aspects of the sexual act parallel inclusion, control, and affection. Inclusion problems refer to the initial phases of the act, the feelings about penetration. If I were a male with problems of inclusion generally, I would probably have erection difficulties. My conflict over whether to penetrate would be reflected in the enervation of my penis and its unwillingness to enter. If I were a woman with inclusion problems my tight, dry vagina would reflect my unwillingness to receive the penis.

Breathing is also primarily an inclusion phenomenon. If I do not want to get involved, I constrict my breathing by tightening my muscles, thus curtailing virtually all vital functions. For centuries, the yogis have recognized the importance of breathing control, pranayama. Breathing is the key to full involvement. For this reason, when I am lecturing or demonstrating to a group, I begin with some activity that requires the audience to breathe deeply, such as screaming, pounding, deep breathing, or anything that gets them pumped up. The result is a much more attentive audience.

The same holds true for an actual encounter group. Activity requiring deep breathing almost invariably will bring an uninvolved member back into the group. Breathing patterns become ingrained early in life, and most people are usually not aware that they do not breathe fully. Improving the breathing pattern is one of the fastest ways to change the feeling of the entire organism.

Hence, the problem of inclusion is *in or out,* the interaction centers on *encounter,* and the physical aspect is that of *energy.*

Control

Control behavior refers to the decision-making process between people in the areas of power, influence, and authority. The need for control varies along a continuum from my desire for authority over others (and therefore over

41

my future) to my need to be controlled and have responsibility lifted from myself.

The example of an argument may help to distinguish the inclusion-seeker from the control-seeker. If I seek inclusion or prominence, I want to be one of the participants in the argument; if I seek control, I want to be a winner or to be on the same side as the winner. If forced to choose, the prominence-seeker would prefer to be a losing participant, while the dominance-seeker would prefer to be a winning nonparticipant.

Control is also manifested in behavior directed toward people who try to control. My expression of independence and rebellion exemplify my lack of willingness to be controlled, while compliance, submission, and taking orders indicate various degrees of my accepting control. There is no necessary relation between my behavior toward controlling others and my behavior toward being controlled. Sergeants may dominate their subordinates, for example, and also accept orders from their lieutenants with pleasure and gratefulness, while neighborhood bullies may dominate their peers and also rebel against their parents.

Control behavior differs from inclusion behavior in that it does not require prominence. The power behind the throne is an excellent example of a role that would simultaneously fulfill a high control need and a low need for inclusion. The comedian exemplifies a high-inclusion person with a low need for control. Control behavior differs from affection behavior in that control is concerned primarily with power relations rather than with emotional closeness.

Control problems usually follow those of inclusion in the development of a group and in interpersonal relationships. Once the group has formed, it begins to differentiate. Different people take or seek different roles, and often power struggles, competition, and influence become central issues. In terms of interaction, these issues usually become matters of confrontation.

If I am an *abdicrat,* a person too low on control, I tend to submit and to abdicate my power. I gravitate toward a subordinate position where I will not have to take responsibility for making decisions. I consciously want other people to relieve me of my obligations. I do not control others even when I should; for example, I would not take charge even during a fire in a children's schoolhouse in which I were the only adult. I never make a decision if I can refer it to someone else.

If I am an *autocrat,* a person too high on control, I am dominating in the extreme. I am a power-seeker, a competitor. I am afraid that others will not be influenced by me, that they will, in fact, dominate me. My underlying feeling is the same as that of the abdicrat: I am not capable of discharging obligation. To compensate for this feeling, I often try to keep proving that I am capable by taking on too much responsibility.

If I am a *democrat,* that is, if in my childhood I successfully resolved my relations in the control area, power and control present no problem. I feel comfortable giving or not giving orders, taking or not taking orders, whichever is appropriate to the situation. Unlike the abdicrat and the autocrat, I am not preoccupied with fears of my own helplessness, stupidity, or incompetence. I feel my competence and am confident that other people trust my ability to make decisions.

The physical concomitants of control behavior include control of the muscles. Males express a great deal of their attitudes toward control in the formation of their upper arms, shoulders, and neck. Hulking, heavily developed shoulders and neck and back muscles frequently reflect a striving for masculinity. Wrestlers and football linemen typify this muscular development in the extreme. The trapezius, the large muscle that extends from the middle of the back up into the neck, is so overdeveloped that it often appears that there is no neck.

In general, my pattern of muscle tensions represents my defense pattern. It is the way in which I control myself so that I can cope with the world. A lack of chronic muscle tensions may indicate a nondefensive state, something like the egolessness of the Eastern mystics.

Feldenkrais (1949) has a novel concept of the relation of the core of the body, the head and spinal column, to the envelope, the pelvic and shoulder girdles and their attached appendages, the legs and arms. His idea is that the core represents *being,* the envelope, *doing.* Most people develop one more than the other.

Intellectual control involves voluntary shaping of the body's propensities. Control is exercised over the body's desires by moral codes so that thought is used to govern action.

In the interaction between myself and my body, the control problem is one of centering. If my body is undercontrolled, it is disorganized; if it is overcontrolled, it is rigid. If my body is well-controlled, its parts are integrated, flowing easily and appropriately. Inappropriate movement and coordination result when my body is unaware of what it is doing, or uncertain of what it wants to do. When I am centered, all my parts are in place and functioning properly. I am "hooked up."

The aspects of the sexual act related to control are the occasion and timing of the orgasms and the movement of the body. Withholding an orgasm is an act of personal control that often has a hostile motive: "You can't satisfy me." Sexual control problems include difficulty of orgasm, premature ejaculation, and lack of ability to let go.

The problem of control is *top or bottom,* the primary interaction is *confrontation,* and the physical aspect is that of *centering.*

Affection

Affection behavior refers to close, personal, emotional feelings between two people. Affection is a dyadic relation; that is, it occurs between pairs of people whereas both inclusion and control relations may occur either in dyads or between one person and a group of persons.

Since affection is based on building emotional ties, it is usually the last phase to emerge in the development of a human relation or of a group. In the inclusion phase, people encounter each other and decide whether to continue their relation; control issues lead them to confront one another and to work out how they will relate. As the relation continues, if affection ties form, people either literally or figuratively embrace.

If I am an *underpersonal,* one who expresses and receives too little affection, I tend to avoid close ties with others. I maintain one-to-one relations on a superficial, distant level and am most comfortable when others do the same with me. I consciously wish to maintain emotional distance and frequently express a desire not to become emotionally involved, while unconsciously I seek a satisfactory affectional relation. My fear is that no one loves me, and in a group situation, I am afraid I will not be liked. I have great difficulty genuinely liking people, and I distrust their feelings toward me.

My attitude could be summarized: "I find the affection area very painful since I have been rejected; therefore, I shall avoid close personal relations in the future." My direct technique as an underspersonal is to avoid emotional closeness or involvement, even to the point of being antagonistic. My subtle technique is to be superficially friendly to everyone. This behavior of mine acts as a safeguard against becoming close to any one person.

My self-concept is that I am unlovable. In contrast to the inclusion anxiety that I am worthless and empty and to the control anxiety that I am stupid and irresponsible, the affection anxiety is that I am nasty and unlovable.

If I am an *overpersonal,* I seek to become extremely close to others, and I want others to seek to be close to me. The unconscious feeling on which I operate is, "My first experiences with affection were painful, but perhaps, if I try again, they will turn out to be better." Being liked is essential to my attempt to relieve anxiety about being rejected and unloved. My direct technique for being liked is to attempt overtly to gain approval, to be extremely personal, ingratiating, intimate, and confiding. My subtle technique, more manipulative and possessive, is to devour friends and subtly punish any attempts by them to establish other friendships.

If I am a *personal,* one who successfully resolved affection relations in childhood, close emotional interaction with another person presents no problem. I am comfortable in a close personal relation as well as in a situation requiring emotional distance. It is important for me to be liked, but if I am not, I can accept that the dislike is the result of the relation between me and the other person; in other words, the dislike does not mean that I am an unlovable person. I am capable of giving genuine affection.

The primary interaction of the affection area is that of embrace, either literal or symbolic. The expression of appropriate deeper feelings is the major issue, particularly in a group situation: at the beginning of the group, there are many statements about how difficult it is to express hostility to people. Most people are surprised to find that it is even more difficult to express warm, positive feelings.

The affection aspect of the sexual act is the feeling that follows its completion. This can be anything from a flood of warm, affectionate, loving feelings to revulsion and thoughts of "What am I doing here?" It depends partly on how well the heart and genitals are connected. The circulatory (heart) and reproductive (genital) system are most directly related to the area of affection.

In the interaction between myself and my body, the affection problem is one of acceptance. My body may be charged with energy (inclusion) and coordinated through centering (control), but the problem of body acceptance remains. When I accept my body, I can allow feeling to flow through all of it. My sensation is not blocked. When I do not accept my body, it works against itself, trying to become sickly or dissociated. Ideally, my body feels energetic, centered, and acceptable.

With respect to interpersonal relations, inclusion is concerned primarily with the formation of a relation, whereas control and affection are concerned with relations already formed. Within existent relations, control is the area concerned with who gives orders and makes decisions, whereas affection is concerned with how emotionally close or distant the relation becomes.

In summary, the problem of affection is *close or distant,* the interaction is *embrace,* and the physical aspect is *acceptance.*

Psychoanalytic Theorists

One way to understand and to reconcile the differences between the three major early psychoanalytic figures, Freud, Adler, and Jung, is to relate them to the FIRO theory.

Perhaps each of these theorists saw most clearly one of the three dimensions and made that dimension his central concern. The keystone for Freud was the libido, sexual energy, and its expression and sublimation. It was the chief theoretical point on which both Adler and Jung departed. In my terms, sexual energy is most prominent in the affection area, although, of course, it has effects in the other two areas as well.

Adler chose to focus his theory on the will to power. In my terms, Adler was emphasizing the control area, the dimension that deals with power, authority, and competition.

Jung's core concept is our relation to nature. He was concerned with mysticism and archetypes that show our continuity with the universe. His primary psychological dimension was introversion-extroversion, almost identical to my in-out, or inclusion, dimension.

All three men had ways of accounting for phenomena in the other two areas. It seems helpful as a way of integrating their approaches to consider that each felt that a different one of the three dimensions was central: for Freud, affection; for Adler, control; for Jung, inclusion.

I-Nature

I offer another speculation, both for its own intrinsic interest and to expand the theory to larger units, such as people in nature, much as it has been expanded in recent years to smaller units, such as the body.

I assume that we relate to the natural world along the same dimensions that we do to each other. How then do we relate to nature in the areas of inclusion, control, and affection?

Inclusion issues revolve around the fundamental relation of myself to nature. Do I want to include myself in nature? Do I want to live or die? What role do I play in nature? Am I a mere speck in the universe, or am I one with the cosmos? What is my importance, significance, commitment to life? How worthwhile is it for me to stay in the natural world? The institution that we have created to deal with these issues we call religion.

My control relation to nature involves establishing my influence over the forces of nature, and my dependence on the natural world for survival. I build dwellings for protection from the weather and invent ways to alter nature, to extract materials from the earth, and to produce heat, light, and food. To succeed in this quest, I must understand nature, learn to overcome natural difficulties, and use nature's resources. The institutions we have created to deal with these issues we call science and engineering.

Expressing my feelings toward nature in the affection area involves uniting very personal expressions of union and harmony (or the opposite) with natural phenomena. Sometimes this expression is direct, as when, as an architect, I attempt to harmonize structures with their natural settings, as an artist, I express my perceptions of a landscape, or, as a sculptor, I take materials from the earth and fashion them in my own unique way. This is a one-to-one relation, like the interpersonal aspect of affection, and unlike the bulk of science, which is necessarily a cumulative enterprise. This individualistic self-expression we institutionalize as art.

The institutions established for expressing our relation to nature in the areas of inclusion, control, and affection are religion, science and art.

I-Thou

If we look at the social patterns we establish to regulate our relations with each other in the areas of inclusion, control, and affection, we should find cultural institutions that have arisen to deal with these three issues.

The inclusion area is the one least clear. Our attempts to devise institutions through which we can contact each other, avoid loneliness, and have each other's company are exemplified by fraternal and sororal organizations, mixers, and encounter groups. Organizations such as the Elks, the Shriners, and college sororities frequently exist for a long time without a specified goal. The Shriners, for example, existed for several decades before they chose to support hospitals as a group function. It was as if they had selected an outside activity to justify their existence, thereby allowing them to continue to satisfy their original need to be together. These organizations are not usually oriented toward heterosexual activities.

48

The social patterns we establish to regulate our relations in the control area are institutionalized in a much more obvious way. Politics, economics, and the military are institutions that are concerned with the exercise and distribution of power in legal, financial, and martial forms. It is striking how much more developed are our institutions for dealing with control than are those for dealing with inclusion.

The social patterns we establish to regulate our relations in the affection area center around the institute of marriage. Marriage consists of an elaborate set of conventions specifying the ways in which one-to-one relations in the affection area are to be expressed. Due to the apparent inadequacy of this one pattern to accomodate all human possibilities, many alternatives to marriage have evolved, and the institution itself has come upon hard times. Attempts to deal with the affection problem often conflict with the institutions dealing with power. The law makes the acceptable patterns of affection difficult to alter. Our culture has only begun to acknowledge the legitimacy of homosexual affection; the gay liberation movement and requests for homosexual marriages have focused attention on these issues.

In summary, our culture has established the institutions of fraternal and sororal organizations for inclusion, politics for control, and marriage for affection. The institutions established to deal with issues of control and of heterosexual affection are the most fully developed. Less developed are the institutions that deal with homosexual affection and with inclusion. This may suggest where we are in our development as a civilization and what kind of institutions must evolve if we are to provide institutionally for human needs.

Summary

Table I provides a summary of the various expressions of inclusion, control, and affection.

Table 1: Relations Among Levels

	Inclusion	Control	Affection
Issue	In or out	Top or bottom	Close or distant
Interaction	Encounter	Confront	Embrace
Self-concept	Importance	Competence	Lovability
Body level	Energy	Centering	Acceptance
Sexual response	Potency	Orgasm	Feeling
Physiology (system)	Senses (esp. skin) Respiratory Digestive Excretory	Nervous Muscular Skeletal Endocrine	Reproductive Circulatory Lymphatic
Psychoanalytic theorist	Jung	Adler	Freud
I-Nature	Religion	Science	Art
I-Thou	Fraternal and Sororal organizations	Politics	Marriage

THEORY OF GROUP DEVELOPMENT

These three dimensions, inclusion, control, and affection, in this order, usually predominate in the development of a group. Inclusion problems, such as the decision to be in or out of the group, usually occur first and are followed by control issues (top or bottom) and finally by affection problems (close or distant). This order, of course, is not rigid, but it seems that the nature of group life is such that people tend first to determine whether they want to be in a group, then to find out what place of influence they will occupy, and finally to decide how personally close they will become. Further, within each of these phases, group members seem to concentrate first on their relations to the leader and then on their relations to each other (Schutz, unpublished).

Inclusion Phase

The inclusion phase begins with the formation of the group. As a member of a new group, first you want to find where you fit. This involves being in our out of the group, establishing yourself as a specific individual, and seeing if you are going to be paid attention to or be left behind or ignored. When you are anxious about these issues, you tend to exhibit individual-centered behavior, such as overtalking, extreme withdrawal, exhibitionism, recitation of your biography, and of other previous experience. At the same time, you are concerned with the basic issue of your commitment to the group. You are implicitly deciding to what degree you will become a member of the group — how much investment you will withdraw from your other life commitments to invest in this new relation. You are asking, "How much of myself will I devote to this group? How important will I be in this setting? Will they appreciate who I am and what I can do, or will I be indistinguishable from many others?" This is the problem of identity. You are primarily deciding how much actual contact, interaction, and communication you wish to have.

Your main concerns during this process of group formation are boundary issues, issues that have to do with crossing or not crossing the boundaries of the group, and with belonging to that group. Boundary issues are problems of inclusion.

Characteristic of groups in this phase is the occurrence of what Semrad (1955) has called "goblet issues." The term is taken from cocktail party behavior where people sometimes pick up their cocktail glass, or goblet, and peer through it, using it to size up the other people at the party. Goblet issues are those which, in themselves, are of minor importance to the group members, but which function as vehicles for getting to know one another, especially in relation to the self. Often a goblet issue is made of the first decision confronting a group.

The goblet issue is by no means confined to cocktail parties. The frustrating experience of having groups discuss endlessly topics of little real interest to anyone is common. Each group finds its own goblet issues within its own framework. "The weather" is fairly universal; "rules of procedure" is common in formal groups; "do you know . . . ?" is characteristic for acquaintances from the same location; relating incidents or telling stories has a goblet element for business gatherings; "where are you from?" often serves for military settings. Although these discussions are often pointless in content, through them members usually learn much about one another. As a group member you know better who responds favorably to you, who sees things the way you do, how much you know compared to the others, and how I, as the group leader, react to you. You also have a fair idea of what type of role you can expect to play in the group. Mark Twain apparently overlooked the fact that nobody really *wants* to "do anything about the weather"; people merely want to use it as a topic for sizing up others. Such discussions are inevitable; contrary to outward appearances, they do serve an important function, and groups not permitted this type of testing will search for some other method of obtaining the same information, perhaps using a decision of more importance to the group.

Inclusion — Leader

While the group activity centers on inclusion, as a member your concern with the commitment of me, as the leader, usually precedes your concern with the other members' commitments to the group. You carefully watch my attendance, apparent interest, preparation for group meetings, and punctuality. If I falter, you feel, "If you don't care, why should I?" It is difficult for you to generate interest in the group when you sense my lack of caring.

Another ingredient of your concern is whether I am fully committed to the group; this is one measure of your own safety. A lack of interest on my part implies to you a danger and the necessity for self-protection. This is especially important if you have accepted the idea that you are responsible for yourself.

Inclusion — Member

Following a satisfactory, though not necessarily final, resolution of this relation your concern shifts to the degree of commitment of the other group members. You are alert particularly to the absence of other members, lateness, amount of participation, and the importance to each member of outside activities compared to this group. You are aware of silent and withdrawn members, and of which members have apparently come to watch.

Control Phase

Once the sense of being together in a group is somewhat established, control issues become prominent: decision-making, the sharing of responsibility, and the distribution of power. At this stage, characteristic group behavior includes a struggle for leadership, competition, and discussion of procedure, of decision-making, and of responsibility. As a group member, your primary anxieties at this point center on having too much or too little responsibility and too much or too little influence. You try to establish yourself in the group in such a way that you will have the amount of power and dependency most comfortable for you.

Control — Leader

During the control phase, your first concern is with your relation to me, the leader. Your struggle with me over power, influence, direction, and structure begins in earnest. This struggle takes the form of wanting both to wrest power from me and to make me assume all responsibility for the group's activities and decisions, that is, to tell you what to do. This is the prototype of authority ambivalence. At this stage, your hostility toward me is expressed by your attempting to oust or quiet me, and by your expressing disappointment in the way the group is going and in my ability.

Control — Member

After you resolve sufficiently your control issues with me, your attention is drawn to your feelings of competition with the other group members. You find yourself in a sibling-like struggle for the approval of, and for a special relation with, me. There is the struggle for the control of the group minus me, for informal leadership of group members. Wrestling is a common occurrence at this time. You observe that as individual members try to take over leadership, they are struck down in their bids by the group, and replaced by other aspirants who meet the same fate. Underlying this phenomenon is the unconscious, or at least suppressed, wish for no one to replace me, and the hope that I will eventually take over.

Affection Phase

Following some resolution of these issues of control, affection issues take center stage. The individuals have come together to form a group; they have differentiated themselves with respect to responsibility and power; now they explore the issue of becoming emotionally integrated. At this stage, it is characteristic to see behavior such as expressions of positive feelings, direct personal hostility, jealousies, pairing off, and in general, heightened emotional feeling between pairs of people.

As a group member, your primary anxieties focus on not being liked, on not being close enough to people, and on being too intimate. You are striving to obtain the most

54

comfortable amount of affection interchange and the most comfortable position in regard to initiating and receiving affection. Like Schopenhauer's porcupines, you want to get close enough to receive warmth and yet to stay far enough away to avoid the pain of sharp quills.

Affection — Leader

As in inclusion and control, the first affection issues revolve around me, the group leader; do you like me and do I like you? By the time this phase occurs, you and the other group members have usually built up various kinds of personal attachments to each other and to me. The issues of jealous, unrequited love, exchange of affection, and sexual attraction now dominate. You become more sensitive to the others and to me. A warmer, closer atmosphere emerges, and my every reward, grimace, and movement is subject to personal interpretation.

Affection — Member

The feelings that you and the other group members have for each other dominate the interaction during this phase. The relations built in the group come to fruition, and the warm, personal atmosphere extends to the tender feelings felt toward each other. You do not necessarily like each of the other members nor do they necessarily like you. Your feelings toward each member, however, are deeper, and you feel you can communicate with each one more adequately then you could at the outset of the group.

The group development hypothesis asserts that certain interactional areas are emphasized at certain points in a group's growth. All three areas are always present but not always equally salient. Similarly, some persons do not always go along with the central issue for the group. For certain individuals, a particular dimension will be so personally potent that it will transcend the current group issue. For each person, the area of concern at any one time is the resultant of the problem areas of the individual and those of the group's current phase. A closer approximation of the developmental phenomena is given by the tire-changing model. When a mechanic changes a tire and replaces the wheel, first each bolt is tightened just enough to keep the wheel in place. Then the bolts are tightened further, usually in the same sequence, until the wheel is firmly in place. Finally, each bolt is gone over separately to secure it fast. Like these bolts, the need areas are worked on until they have been resolved sufficiently to allow the group to continue with the work at hand. Later, the need areas are returned to and worked on until they are more satisfactorily resolved. If one bolt was not tightened well in the first cycle, during the next cycle it will receive more attention.

Since all groups have members with interpersonal needs that must be satisfied by the other members, this theory applies to any interpersonal relation. Every time people form themselves into groups, including two-person groups, the same three interpersonal problem areas are dealt with in the same order. In certain social situations external forces may be imposed to alter the manner of handling the problem areas, but they still must be dealt with. In the military organization, for example, the uniform certainly helps to create a feeling of belonging or inclusion. The stripes or bars, on the arm or shoulder, clarify the issues of control and power distribution. Fraternization rules and customs influence the expression of affection. These external factors, however, by no means solve the interpersonal problems. Uniformed soldiers may still feel that they are being ignored as individuals or that they are not being treated as important persons. Sergeants may feel that they should have more influence than their inexperienced lieutenants. A captain may feel that the rules of personal separation for officers and enlisted personnel conflict with the desire to become more intimate with a corporal.

Separation

As groups terminate, they tend to resolve their relations in the opposite sequence, namely affection, control, and inclusion. Groups or relations that are about to terminate or markedly reduce their interaction exhibit fairly characteristic behaviors: absences and latenesses increase; there is more daydreaming; members forget to bring materials to the group; discussion of death and illness is frequent; the importance and goodness of the group is minimized; general involvement decreases; often there is a recall of earlier experiences. As a member of a terminating group, you usually want to discuss with the group the events that were not completely worked through at the time they occurred; in this way, you hope that your relations will be resolved successfully. Often, when you feel that your actions in an earlier meeting were misunderstood, you will recall the instance and explain what you really meant to say, so that no one will be angry with you. Sometimes, you want to express to other members that comments they made earlier were important to you and made you feel better. On it goes, with all unresolved incidents being reworked. After the group members complete this process of reworking unresolved incidents, they are more capable of accepting separation.

In the process of group resolution, the personal positive and negative feelings are dealt with first (affection). Next, the discussion focuses on the leader and on the reasons for compliance with, or rebellion against, the leader's wishes (control). Later come discussions about the possibilities of continuing the group and about how committed each member really was, and finally, about the fact that they all are going into different groups and will no longer be members of the present one (inclusion).

Your responses to impending separation depend upon your major need areas and your preferred methods of coping with anxiety. As a group member, you may respond to impending separation by gradually withdrawing your investment in the group as indicated by your increased absence, lateness, and reduced participation. Or you may disparage and demean the group, as if to say, "You see, I won't miss such an unimportant group." Or you may shift the responsibility for separation onto the other group members by becoming antagonistic and forcing them to reject you. Or separation may be so difficult for you that your method of handling it has become a character trait: You refrain from becoming invested in people from the first time you meet them.

The fantasy reunion is a common group technique. You make elaborate plans to come together in one month, six months, or a year; a paper is circulated to collect names and addresses, and someone volunteers to reproduce the list and send it to everyone. The meeting almost never occurs, but the preparation for it makes the actual separation easier.

Summary

Interpersonal relations, in all groups, regardless of size, seem to deal with the same issues in the same sequence. They start with inclusion, then deal with control, then with affection. As the relation terminates, withdrawal occurs in the reverse order: affection, control, inclusion. Within each of these phases, the group members deal first with relations to the leader, then with their relations to one another. These phases are not discrete, but represent the area of interpersonal interest focused on at a given time.

THE ENCOUNTER GROUP

Groups using the encounter model typically meet in a workshop setting. A workshop is usually a five-day session, although some are designed to last for a weekend, 2 weeks, 4 weeks, 4 months, or 9 months. The workshops are residential; that is, all participants live in the same location during the workshop.

I used to offer once-a-week groups, daily groups, and individual sessions, in a wide variety of patterns from 2 days to 3 years in length. These experiences led me to the conclusion that the depth that can be reached in a concentrated workshop is remarkable compared to the other approaches. I have, therefore, virtually abandoned all other patterns.

It seems to me that an effective path to the realization of your potential is for you to choose your own growth experiences, thus taking responsibility for your own growth. Some people take many intense workshops in succession and then stay away for long intervals to give themselves a chance to assimilate their experiences. Some attend workshops infrequently, but regularly. Others shift the type of experience, say, from encounter to sensory awareness to meditation to massage and perhaps back to encounter. I have found, however, as have others who have reported similar conclusions, that one intensive week is equivalent to two or three years of periodic therapy sessions and that groups are more effective than individual sessions.

Encounter workshops (formerly called "More Joy" workshops) given at Esalen typically start Sunday evening and continue until Friday noon; they meet each day from 10 a.m. to lunch and from 8:30 p.m. until about midnight. The afternoon is free until 4, when there is usually a general session for all groups. A workshop typically has 40 to 60 people in it, broken down into 4 or 5 groups of 10 to 15 people each. Occasionally a group will meet all night. Wednesday night is free, and there is often a dance, a good opportunity for spontaneous physical expression. The week ends Friday at noon with a general session.

Lately, Esalen has been exploring month-long workshops in which participants work at maintenance tasks, such as dishwashing, gardening, and cabin cleaning, as part of the workshop experience. This pattern appears promising. The general assumption is that a total concentrated experience permits breakthroughs and intensity difficult to attain in longer, intermittent, drawn-out patterns. There are, however, advantages to the regular meetings over time, and it remains for group leaders and members to experiment to find the best tempo for themselves.

The past years have seen the growth in popularity of marathons, in which the group meets continuously from 12 to 48 hours, with few or no breaks, and sleeps right in the meeting room. The point of these marathons is to break down defenses through lack of sleep, to get to deeper material faster. Exhaustion does not seem to me, however, to be an effective or necessary way to break down defenses.

Several of the methods described in Schutz (1967, 1971) seem more effective for defense penetration. In marathons, it often happens that important group events happen when many group members are asleep; this erodes the integrity of the group. Yet allowing people a break for sleep may be extremely valuable. Group members often seek out a few persons with whom they have unfinished business, sleep and have important dreams, or have time alone to assimilate what has happened and often come up with important insights and integrations. These advantages seem to outweigh the virtues of staying awake. As a group leader, my effectiveness is greatly diminished when I am tired. My preference, therefore, is to have long meetings to take advantage of the buildup of intensity, but to stop whenever the group's work seems to be done and the members have experienced all they can assimilate. Then they can sleep and return refreshed.

You, as a group member, come voluntarily to a workshop. There is no pre-selection, but a flagrantly disturbed case is usually excluded. My preference is to experience the person in the group setting before making such a judgment. In point of fact, I have virtually never excluded anyone from a group.

The issue of confidentiality is not specifically discussed unless you bring it up. In the initial contract it is stated that you are responsible for yourself. This implies that if you do not want outsiders to know something, you should not say it, or else you must trust the judgment of the others. The encounter group is most effective when you and the other group members feel comfortable saying anything openly and taking responsibility for it, that is, when you reach the point where you are willing to have anything you are, known to anyone. In that direction lies freedom.

The rare exceptions to this dictum usually have to do with pending litigation or some such concern. In these cases, the member concerned typically tells the group, and they respond appropriately. The vow of confidentiality is usually avoided in the group; it is seen as supporting a position of dependency and distrust. The lack of such a vow rarely, if ever, inhibits expression.

Sound or video recordings are sometimes made if there is a specific reason, such as a research project or an exercise in seeing or hearing oneself. Recording without a specific purpose simply leads to closets full of unheard tapes.

The group usually begins without preliminaries, such as interviews, tests (except for research), and physical examinations. The idea of self-responsibility would be negated if an outside judgment were to be imposed on a person's decision to enter the group.

The Rules of Encounter

From the philosophy and theory underlying encounter emerge very specific ways of leading a group; these ways can be expressed as a set of rules for group interaction. The rules have the purpose of implementing the principles stated above: honesty, awareness, responsibility, and body acceptance. In this sense, they constitute an alternate way of dealing with oneself and with other people that is applicable to all aspects of human existence, especially human interaction. These rules constitute the basis of the encounter culture and the guidelines for leading a group.

Encounter rules are conveyed to the group members as a guide for changing from their familiar mode of interaction to the encounter mode. As a group leader, it is important for me to be clear about what this mode is and not to delude myself that I am equally content with whatever happens in the group, or that I am objective. I prefer to be aware of my own leanings and how they affect the way I am in the group. The method by which these rules are conveyed varies with the setting. Any or all of the rules may be stated, modeled, or conveyed by reinforcing or discouraging spontaneous group behavior that conforms to or violates the rules. To illustrate: In an engineering group I had great difficulty getting the members to follow the encounter group model. They appeared at the group meetings with notebooks and clip-boards and expected to hear a lecture on human relations. After fighting this attitude, I decided to capitulate and to take them from where they were. I proceeded to write some rules on the blackboard: talk only about feelings, be open and honest, no back home anecdotes, use first names only. This worked beautifully. They copied these rules eagerly and had great fun following them and conscientiously calling each other on rule violations. Other groups, however, do not react well to such structuring. For them I may use other methods such as reading the rules, letting the rules be known gradually, making a rule clear whenever something relevant to it comes up in the group or by whatever means seems appropriate.

To simplify their presentation, I shall state all rules in the imperative.

The first set of rules establishes open and honest communication:

Be Honest With Everyone, Including Yourself.

In the group, we communicate as openly and honestly as possible; everything that happens outside the group is available to the group on the same basis. Secrets are discouraged; they usually stem from shame. Lying, evasion, and duplicity clog the group process.

Pay Close Attention to Your Body.

It tells you when you're lying, either to someone else or to yourself. Be aware. Use your body signals to keep yourself truthful.

Concentrate on Feelings.

Ideas are often used to hide feelings. Stay in touch with the feeling; the body helps here, too. Thoughts are good mainly to explore a feeling already experienced.

Start with the Here-and-Now.

This helps you to stay with feelings and avoids your going off into safer areas invested with less real emotional energy. The uniqueness of the group is best used by concentrating on the joint experience of group members, those events that occur while we are all present. Usually, one person's account of an outside experience can elicit little more than a round of advice-giving. Outside events are valuable, however, when they derive from the here-and-now. If, for example, you are told in the group that you are weak, it may remind you that the same comment was made by your spouse. You can continue to learn more about your marital situation by using the group. For example, you may ask the group members of the opposite sex to react to you as if they were your spouse. In this situation, they are responding to your marital situation from their own firsthand experience with you, instead of simply giving you advice based on your one-sided report of an outside event.

The next set of rules focuses on the body, integrating the body into the group activity:

Meet in Rooms and in Clothes That Allow Maximum Freedom of Movement.

The ideal room has only a rug and pillows on the floor. Chairs anchor people, and tables place barriers between them and hide their bottom halves. Padded walls are desirable. Sharp or excessively hard objects, such as radiators, are not. This provides a safe surrounding for maximum physical mobility. Wear unrestricting clothing; avoid encumbering clothing such as jackets, purses, shawls, and shoes.

Sit or Stand in a Position Such That You Can Move Toward Any Other Person Easily.

This creates conditions conducive to movement and physical contact. To sit in distant locations, such as against opposite walls, is to lose this advantage.

Don't Drink Coffee or Eat During a Meeting.

Coffee and food serve as undesirable diversions and dissipate much of the energy a group has generated.

Whenever There Is an Opportunity to Express Something Physically, Rather Than Verbally, Do It Physically.

Use your whole body to express your feelings, instead of just talking about them. Tears, bruises, scratches, sore muscles are always possible and rarely serious.

Fight When It Feels Right.

When there is a fight, stand in front of windows, sharp or hard objects, or anything in the room that might cause damage, and fend off the antagonists. Men are encouraged to wrestle rather than fight with their fists, and it is a little safer if both start in a kneeling position. But these limits are open to negotiation. If both men want to use fists or start upright, that may be all right. Remember, you are responsible for yourself and what happens to you. The risk of physical injury has proved negligible in encounter experience, and compared to the important feelings that are generated by physical contact such as fighting unfought fights, dealing with physical fear, and testing strength, it is extremely worthwhile.

Take Off Your Clothes When It Feels Right.

Nudity is valuable for working on body image and body acceptance. In our culture, there is a great taboo on nudity. Transcending the taboo on nudity often leads to important breakthroughs, and bodies turn out to be more beautiful than most people imagine.

Don't Smoke.

Smoking reduces tensions that would be more useful if they were brought out and worked on in the group. Be aware of when you want to smoke and of what anxiety is giving rise to the desire.

Don't Take Drugs.

Bring your tensions to the group. Aspirin, alcohol, marijuana, tranquilizers, or any other drugs designed to alleviate anxiety or pain, except, of course, in extreme cases, should be avoided. Body ailments are assumed to be self-inflicted and are better dealt with than masked.

Don't Wear Glasses or Contact Lenses.

If you have a serious identified, physical defect, this does not apply to you. If often happens that during the course of a week-long workshop, a glasses-wearer will experience a brief moment of perfect vision. If you object that you can not see people if you take off your glasses, move close enough to others that you can see them. This may help you to find out what function is being served by your not letting yourself see better. When you remove your glasses you also remove a physical barrier.

To establish your identity and to encourage you to take responsibility for yourself, several other rules are helpful:

Take Responsibility for Yourself.

You are responsible for yourself and for whatever happens to you. It's your choice whether you attend the group or not, whether you bow to pressure or resist it, whether you go crazy, are bored, get physically injured, learn something, stay or leave, or whatever. It's up to you. Your personal responsibility also includes "accidents," unconscious behavior, body attitudes, and many other individual productions.

Make Statements.

Questions are discouraged in favor of the statements that almost invariably underlie them. Most of your questions are statements for which you are not taking responsibility. For instance, "Are all groups so slow in getting started?" often means, "I am afraid that you are disappointed in me," or perhaps, "You are a rotten leader." You are encouraged to make the statement, and to make it directly to the person toward whom you have the feeling. There are some legitimate questions, but not many. An exception is made for leaders at the beginning of a group when they are trying to convey the desired structure of the group. But if they keep it up too long, they too are defending.

Take Responsibility for Your Choices.

Your word habits often reflect failure to take responsibility for your feelings and behavior. "Can't" is discouraged; replace it with "won't." The statement, "I can't make it to the meeting today," and its variation, "I'm too busy," are almost never true. It is more accurate to say, "I choose to do something else rather than to meet with you." The use of "can't" implies a force in the universe beyond your control, whereas in fact you are in control of virtually all of your actions. By using the word "can't," you avoid taking responsibility for what you choose to do. The phrase "I don't know" is also discouraged. It usually means, "I don't want to think about it any more," or, "I might not like what I (or you) will find out if I pursue it further," (a frequent reason behind "no comment" in press conferences or law courts). In one example, "I don't know" was given as an answer to the question, "Why did you forget to pack my lunch?" Probing revealed that the respondent did indeed know, and that the answer, "I was mad at you for what you did last night," unveiled a situation that she could avoid facing by saying "I don't know." Probe deeper. You are urged to think more and give another answer. "If you did know, what would it be?", or "If you had to give two answers and the first was 'I don't know,' what would the second be?"

Speak for Yourself.

Avoid general phrases that imply popular support for a personal feeling. Such phrases include, "People always . . . ," "Whenever you are in a situation you . . . ," "We feel . . . ," "It's only human nature to . . . ," "The group feels . . . ," These phrases usually mean, "*I* feel." By saying "people" or "we," you imply that yours is a common response, not unique to you. There is safety in numbers. Usually you have no idea how "we," or "people," or "the group" feel. All you really know is your own feeling. Interviews after big events are full of these general phrases, for example: "How does it feel to finally win the Super Bowl, Sherm?" "Well, when you've lost before, it's natural to get discouraged. People have to regain confidence in themselves, so when you finally do win, it feels awfully good . . ." Speak for yourself and take personal responsibility by saying "I feel . . ."

Speak Directly to the Person Addressed.

Too frequently, group members will say, "Harold always looks so happy," when Harold is sitting right there. The communication is more meaningful if Harold is faced and spoken to directly instead of talked about as if he were absent.

Don't Use Globalisms.

These are statements, often jargon, so broad that they make doing anything about them very difficult. Examples are: "I just want to be me"; "I have trouble with interpersonal relations"; "I have a father complex"; "I can't communicate with people"; "I want to be real." The broad statement does not allow for anything specific to follow, and, further, it usually hides a much simpler and more usable feeling. For example, "Man is inherently evil," may mean, "He rejected me last night and I am very hurt and angry."

Avoid Non-committal Words.

Several words sound as if they convey meaning, but most of the feeling is hidden. Such words include "interested," "surprised," "curious," "different," "strange," and "funny." If, for example, you say, "I'm just here because I'm curious," you communicate little feeling unless you also state whether you feel frightened, exhilarated, disdainful, or whatever.

67

If Something Is Happening That You Don't Like, Take Responsibility For Doing Something About It.

If you are bored and you don't want to be, do something so you won't be bored. The same holds for any unwanted feeling you are experiencing. It is up to you to change it.

If you find yourself bored or experiencing any other negative feeling, try to find out what it is you do that brings out the boring (or irritating, or dominating, or self-pitying, or otherwise unpleasing) parts of people. A man in a couples group complained that his wife was always creating crises in their marriage. As he worked on it, it became apparent that whenever the marriage was going well he started withdrawing and going elsewhere. Only when there was a crisis would he give attention and energy to his wife. In other words, he rewarded the very thing he complained of. Eliciting apparently unwanted behavior is a common phenomenon.

The use of body energy to help expand the limits of the self-concept gives rise to two important rules:

If You Are Saying Something About Yourself That You Have Said Before, Stop, and Say Something Else.

These repetitions create a sense of *cold potatoes* because the feeling behind the account is hollow and without much energy. If this is a recounted tale, for instance something you have already told a psychoanalyst, then you are probably hiding something of greater importance. You can become familiar with whether or not your language has any energy behind it. Try saying the opposite. For example, if, once again, you find yourself saying that you always want to resist the leader, explore how much you want the leader to tell you what to do. This is especially useful for veteran group members, "encounter bums," who have devised elaborate systems for attending many groups and profiting from none.

Do Whatever You Are Most Afraid of Doing.

The experience of being afraid is the signal that you feel that the limit of your self-concept has been reached. This is true whether the fear is elicited by combating a strong man, professing your attraction to a woman, challenging the leader, making a fool of yourself in front of the group, taking off your clothes, singing in public, or whatever. If you go beyond this limit, you are likely to experience a feeling of freedom.

The Encounter Group Leader

When I first considered what to call the person who runs the group, the term group leader sounded too stark and military; it did not convey the more participative, democratic elements of the process. Many names had been suggested, but each seemed to fall short. "Trainer" sounds too much like a lion tamer; "coordinator," too much like a telephone operator; "agent," too much like James Bond. "Facilitator" is true enough, but a little thin. Calling the leader just another group member is hypocritical. "Clarifier," one who helps people to be non-deceptive is good, but then, in thinking about the concept of a leader, it occurred to me that I would like all leaders to have the qualities of a good encounter group leader.

The ideal group leader is self-aware, creates an atmosphere in which feelings are recognized and expressed easily, and senses what the group needs and causes it to be provided, be it strong direction, passivity, information, or energy. Hence I chose the term encounter group leader.

The encounter group provides multiple transference objects and, therefore, makes it easier for many deep feelings to be aroused. This suggests some principles for group composition. Parent-child transference is more likely to occur in a group with persons of various ages than in one-to-one psychotherapy. Transference toward me, as the leader, is one reason I make my own reality known to the group. The valuable part of working with transference is that when you, as a group member, are the person transferring, you can learn about your distorted perceptions and, perhaps, minimize them. The discrepancy between the way you see me and the way I really am, is due to your unresolved infantile conflicts. For example, you, as a female group member, may perceive me, the leader, as physically attracted to you and as acting seductively. You may be projecting because you always wanted your father to feel seductive toward you, or it may be that, in fact, I am physically attracted to you and I am acting seductively. If I am not willing and able to reveal my own feelings in this situation, I may cause you unjustified concern about your need to see authority figures as attempting to seduce you.

Countertransference is subject to similar distortion unless I am aware of my feelings and willing to express them. When I do have feelings that cause me inner conflict, such as sexual attraction or hostility to certain group members, it is important that I reveal them to the group. Otherwise my behavior will seem obtuse to the group. In some groups, there are times when I do not like certain group members and have no desire whatever to help them. On the contrary, I might have an urge to be sarcastic and cynical. One woman, in a recent group, played directly into an unresolved prejudice of mine. I felt she was rigid, old, righteous, self-deceptively destructive, and hypocritical. Whenever she had an interchange with another member, I wanted to make her realize how stupid and evil she was. Soon my body tensions signaled me that I was in one of my own areas of difficulty and that I had best be careful. Since I noticed that a nurse in the group had a more benign feeling toward the woman, I invited the nurse to take over and I simply supported what she did.

When I am the group leader, I often perceive persons who threaten me as saying irrelevant things, which I, therefore, ignore, put down, or interrupt in order to return to something else; persons I want to impress find me very showy and preening.

These feelings can clutter a group, and it is important to be constantly aware of them. When I detect such a feeling in myself, I find it best to inform the group members and ask them to be aware of it. This often leads the group to put a check on me and leads me to become more objective, or to confront and work out my feelings.

The qualities that make a good group leader also make a good helper. In encounter groups, as in life generally, the ability to help someone is very complex and requires far more than simply a soothing hug when someone is crying. A hug is sometimes the most unhelpful thing a person can do. In a professional group at a state hospital, one social worker

70

began to express great concern over her incompetence. A psychologist, abetted by several other group members, immediately reassured her that he felt she was unusually competent, that everyone liked her, and that she was doing wonderful work. Her tears stopped in a few minutes, and she managed a brave smile of gratitude. At the next meeting, she arrived very angry. "My feelings were cut off yesterday," she said. She still felt incompetent and had not had a chance to ventilate all her feelings. She felt that reassurance had been provided by people who did not know her faults, which she had been denied the opportunity to describe and explore. She resented their attempt to put a bandaid on a festering sore.

In groups, I have the most difficulty when a problem arises that is similar to one of my own. As I work through problems of my own in each area, I am far better able to allow and to help group members to work through their problems in that area. This is true of problems such as loneliness, dependence, anger, hetero- and homosexuality, competence, nudity, money, masculinity, and worthlessness.

It is sometimes difficult for me to recognize the close connection between my own problems and my limits as a leader. Failure to do so may lead me into complex rationalizations about why groups or individuals should not enter into my problem areas. Sometimes leaders' limitations are institutionalized through rules called professional ethics.

Administrative considerations often contaminate therapeutic efficacy. Many group leaders feel that fighting in groups, for instance, is dangerous because injury and lawsuits may follow. Theirs is, indeed, a legitimate concern. It is unfortunate, however, to rationalize that concern in therapeutic terms such as, "I don't allow fighting because it is acting out / is not necessary / has no point / encourages aggression / and so on." Each of these reasons may at times be true. In my experience, however, there have been many instances when fighting was of great therapeutic value. For me to say I do not allow fighting because I fear a lawsuit seems an honest, legitimate choice. But for me to say that fighting is always therapeutically worthless seems objectively questionable and indicates my lack of self-awareness.

The same is true for sexuality. The clearer I am about my own feelings, the more effective I am in letting group members work in any sexual area deeply and as riskily as is necessary for them to work through their problems.

Leader Technique: Follow the Energy

One of the most important phenomena to which a group leader must become sensitive is energy, both group and individual. As a leader, I am most effective when I follow the energy.

A look around an encounter group will reveal people in very different states. Some are in a relaxed state; they have no pressing issue. If the group focuses on these people, the result is usually a dull and lifeless interchange without feeling or energy. Vital group interactions happen when the group goes to where the energy is. If you, as a member, are holding yourself tight, I, as the leader, may either move on to someone else and count on the group interaction to loosen you up so that you can work better later, or I may choose to try now to help you to break through that defense. My first step might be to ask you to relax by unlocking your arms and legs, if you have them crossed, by standing up and shaking yourself loose, or by jiggling and breathing deeply for several minutes. If a particular part of your body seems tight, either I or a group member might massage it. From this point on, I pay attention to how your body responds as you talk and act. I assume the feeling is focused where there is tightening or jiggling, and that is where it will be most valuable to work.

Sometimes you may be wound up too tight to be able to function. In this case, I encourage you to do something physical, such as beat on some pillows or scream. This action helps to drain off enough energy so that you can begin to work with the real problem. If the issue seems to be competition, a wrestling match, or at least an arm wrestle, may help mobilize and focus the energy. The strength of your anger, jealousy, or competition may become apparent when your whole body is involved in combat, whereas sitting and talking allows you to hide this feeling from yourself.

You may be ready to work in a group, but need support. When you clear your throat, it often means that you want to say something, but you inhibit yourself. Throat-clearing often functions as a request for attention. Or you may ask for support by looking depressed, by crying, by withdrawing, by making sarcastic comments, or by any behavior that calls attention to yourself. My interest and initiative may be sufficient to help you start to deal with your held-in energy.

Once you start to work, that is, to talk or act on an issue, I keep an eye on your energy. You may start to work, then begin to intellectualize, at which point the tone of your voice will change from one filled with emotion to one that is casual and controlled. Some of your visible body tension will dissipate or go deeper into your body.

Bullshit (the technical term for talk unconnected to feeling) is frequently a good fertilizer and makes other material grow more fully. It may permit a more full-blown working-through and may also give me clues where to go next with the emerging material. The focus on the energy must be maintained, however, or defenses may take over and the value of the work will be dissipated. An inexperienced leader often falls prey to the *green apples* phenomenon. When I was a new leader, in my eagerness to test out my abilities I often seized the first feeling presented in the group and started to work on it with great flourish and virtuosity. The difficulty was that I frequently chose a shallow feeling not attached to much energy; after the first exchange, the feeling was gone and the action degenerated into shallow wordiness. My choice to pursue a given opening is better made after getting a sense that the apple is ripe, that the feelings being expressed are deep and backed by significant energy. Dull groups result from the pursuit of energyless issues.

As I become more skilled, more happens in my groups with less effort on my part. When I am sensitive to where in the group the energy and feeling lie, I can help the group to focus its energy on them. Then every group event is meaningful and valuable. As others work through deep feelings, the group becomes a safer place in which to work. If you, a timid member, see others working ineffectually and with less feeling than you know you have inside yourself, the group will seem an unsafe place for you. Your feelings are deep, and you have no assurance that feelings of such depth can be dealt with in this group.

Energy also indicates when a person has finished working on a problem. When you really have resolved an issue, your energy is discharged, your body relaxed. Completion can be checked by observing your body; does it look relaxed, or are there still some parts that are tight? Are you still jiggling or picking at the carpet? Is your voice tight or relaxed? Does your face look relaxed, or is it still tight? Is your breathing full or shallow? These and other clues tell when the issue is resolved, and the indicators are usually quite clear. It is important to follow through until you are fully relaxed. If you still seem tense, even though you appear finished, I will encourage you to continue; usually, this will help you explore the issue in greater depth.

The concept of energy clarifies how substances such as cigarettes, aspirin, and alcohol impede group progress. They dissipate energy and therefore prevent its use in a profitable way. When you desire these aids it is likely that your anxiety is aroused. Smoking and drinking flatten feeling. In a recent group, a girl started to light up a cigarette at the end of a meeting. I asked her what she might be anxious about.

"Nothing," she replied. "I always light up when I feel relaxed. I've been smoking for years. It's just a habit."

"Anything happen in the meeting that might have upset you?"

"No, it was a very nice session."

"Were you attracted to anyone in the group?" I thought I had detected a flirtation.

"Well, yes — one young man."

"Was he attracted to you?"

"I don't know." Her voice dropped.

"Who is it?"

She pointed to a young man who was just lighting up a cigarette.

As this vignette unfolded, the anxiety around the possible unrequited attraction became obvious, and the significance of the cigarette as an indicator became apparent. Had she simply finished her cigarette, her anxiety might have been alleviated sufficiently that she need not have dealt with her attraction, and perhaps she would have been able to keep her anxiety out of her awareness. When I walk into an encounter group that is enshrouded in cigarette smoke, I expect that nothing of much significance is happening: much of the usable energy of the group has gone up in smoke.

As an energy cycle is completed, I look around the group for clues where to go next. The cycle has probably affected many members. I focus on the persons with the most energy. This helps maintain a high level of energy in the group as a whole.

The concept of energy clarifies the group decision-making process. In making a decision, the group goes through an energy cycle. The completion of this cycle is indicated by the body relaxation of each group member. If such relaxation has not occurred, the group is not fully ready to implement its decision, and retrogression may occur. Completion of an energy cycle usually will make a permanent change in a person, and in a group.

To ascertain whether the group members are ready to go along with a decision, I ask the members individually and note their reactions. Any response other than a clear "yes" almost always means, "No, I'm not yet ready to go along with the decision."

Unreadiness to go along may be indicated by any occurrence that prevents an easy flow of the decision-making process. Expressions such as, "Would you repeat the decision again?" "I don't understand the question," "It's time for lunch," as well as nonverbal cues of discomfort or boredom, may indicate unreadiness. If this unreadiness is ignored, a decision may be reached more quickly. This speed, however, is illusory, since compliance with the decision is far slower.

When I detect your unreadiness, I encourage you to discuss your objections more fully. When you feel that your position has been understood and your feelings have been acknowledged, and you see that the group still opposes you, usually you are willing to acquiesce, even though you still personally disagree. At this point, the group energy cycle is complete and each member is ready to comply. This situation is known as group consensus. Often, however, discussion of the dissenting view may influence other members to change their minds. You may be voicing a feeling that lay dormant in them. An excellent example of this process occurs in the movie *Twelve Angry Men*, in which the one juror who holds out gradually persuades the other eleven to switch.

When you fail to recognize the first feeling that occurs to you in response to some action, and you act instead on a second feeling, usually a defense, communication becomes distorted. In a recent group one person said to another, "I think what you just did was phony," to which the second replied, "Well, if you didn't like it, why didn't you stop me?"

"I didn't stop you because it's not up to me to teach you how to behave."

Since the first feeling was omitted from each statement, their verbalizing grew more and more irrelevent. If each man had been in touch with his first feeling, the interchange might have gone like this:

"I think what you did was phony."

"I feel hurt when you say that, then I feel angry."

"I'm sad that it hurts you. I don't want you to dislike me."

The next interchange might have gone like this:

"Well, if you didn't like it, why didn't you stop me?"

"I feel guilty when you say that. I feel as you do. I feel sad and despondent. I feel that I never speak up when I should."

The overlooked feelings of hurt in the first case,- and of guilt and sadness in the second, were the first feelings. The anger and debating were defensive reactions to hide the first feelings. Since the interchange continued at this defensive level, it remained relatively unproductive. Had the focus been directed to the first feelings, each of the men might have become aware of them, and the words and feelings would have been congruent. This is an example of productive verbalizing. The first interchange is an example of bullshit.

The use of nonverbal methods may rob you of your verbal defenses. When talk seems to be making things less clear, I may ask the principals to continue communicating, but without words. When the anger is high, you may fight. At other times you may hug, shake hands, or turn your back. When nonverbal techniques are used, real feeling tends to emerge spontaneously.

When the first feeling is ignored, the interaction that follows may have a phony, wheel-spinning quality. A technique for redirecting the focus to the first feeling is to follow non-verbal cues, such as facial expressions, postures, and breathing. Ignoring first feelings is a frequent source of marital difficulties. One husband always came home and made an offhand remark to his wife, who then started nagging. When this situation was examined, it turned out that she felt he often belittled her intelligence. Not having gone to college, she was very sensitive about her intelligence. Her response was deep hurt, of which she was unaware. Her defense was to put him down at every opportunity, as if to say, "You see, you're not so smart either." When he became aware that he was hurting her, his whole attitude toward her changed, as did her attitude toward him. They were able to turn a fighting situation into one of mutual exploration; this transformation is a crucial turning point for any couple. When the energy is directed to the first feeling, there is frequently an exchange of human warmth previously prevented by defensive behavior. One man had a fixed smile that irritated almost everyone. He was phony, unreachable, and saccharine, and many members simply withdrew from him. When he dropped his smile, the sadness behind it became obvious to the others. Their feeling of irritation changed to a desire for emotional and physical closeness. He relaxed and started to confide some of his fears about the present situation. Others were empathizing. These were feelings that they could recognize personally, and they began to feel closer to him.

Energy is manifest in an ineffable, but often tangible, way. You can learn to become sensitive to energy fields that surround everyone. There has long been an unconscious awareness of these fields. They are only now beginning to be scientifically measurable (see Gallert, 1966; Ostrander and Schroeder, 1971; and Kilner, 1965, on the measurement of human auras).

To assess quickly where a group is in its development, I use methods that combine energy fields, non-verbal behavior, and the concepts of inclusion, control, and affection. To assess group inclusion, I ask the group members to walk around the room silently, without trying to "figure out" what they want to do, until they find the place that feels most comfortable to them. This exercise quickly reveals who feels in the group and who feels out. Some members drift toward the corner, some seek the center; some turn their backs, some face one person and shun others; subgroups form. The important element of this exercise is the elimination of thinking and the use of body feeling to lead to the place of comfort and to avoid the places of discomfort. In terms of energy, this process focuses on the interaction of the energy fields of the group members. Compatible members draw each other close, and incompatible members repel each other.

The dominance line is an excellent procedure for assessing the control energies in the group. My instructions are, "Without thinking about it and without words, arrange yourselves in a straight line. If you feel that you are a dominant person, go to the head of the line, and if you feel you are a submissive person go to the back of the line. Find what feels like your proper place. If others are already there, feel free to remove them." Scuffles often break out in the front or even in the middle of the line. Some members back away and some wait until the fighting stops, then sneak in at the front. Control relations become clear through the use of aggressive energy.

To assess the affection area, I suggest, "silently look into each other's eyes, then simultaneously explore each other's faces with your hands." This intimacy immediately informs both me and you how the others feel about you. You may hug; you may feel energy merge with that of others; you may experience fear and hastily go on to the next face; you may become detached and begin an exploration of facial anatomy. However you react, your affection feelings become clearer to me.

Thus, in 20 to 30 minutes, by using body energies and by blocking out verbalizing and cerebrating, it is possible to obtain a clear notion of where a group stands with regard to each of the three interpersonal areas.

As the group explores deeper feelings, it develops a feeling of the unity of humanity. When a group is allowed to stay at the level of defenses, the amount of human exchange is minimal and superficial, as at a cocktail party. As defenses are penetrated, there is the dawning recognition of the universality of the human condition, of the sameness of human needs, fears, and hopes. Criticism of others seems pointless, and the search for a mutual accommodation begins. Deep hatred toward anyone is very difficult to maintain when you are encountering that person. This does not mean that you will like everyone whom you encounter at this deep level. It means, rather, that your understanding is greatly increased and your fear reduced.

Although it may seem paradoxical, deeper groups are safer groups. When a group has shared deep feelings, the closeness that results provides you someone to go to, a friend, a roommate, a group member, should you find yourself in emotional difficulty. The sharing of humanity, the energy that comes from the center of each member, often gives this phase of a group a mystical or spiritual quality. As the feeling of the unity of humankind becomes a reality, the members who looked so strange, alien, and undesirable at the beginning of the group unfold into people who share with you the same psychological underworld.

Case Example

In order to make these theoretical ideas more concrete, I shall present an example of some work done in a recent group in which I was the leader It illustrates a variety of methods and provides an example of changing from one method to another to follow the energy as it moves, both within the group and within the individual.

Peony joined a 5-day group of 12 members, some with group experience and some without. Peony was an attractive, 27-year old woman. She had come to the group with her male friend because she wanted to learn about groups, to improve her relation with her friend, and to feel more comfortable around other people. She had grown up in a small town in England and had become more experienced and comfortable with nature and animals than with people.

By the fourth day, she had said barely a word, but seemed quite content with her passive role. No one in the group had made any attempt to bring her out. Helen, another group member, began working on a problem with her mother, using a gestalt-psychodramatic technique. Helen let a pillow represent her mother and expressed her resentment at being pushed away from her mother too early. She became angry, pounded the pillow, cried, changed roles and became her mother; then, as "mother," she explained to "Helen" (the pillow) the problem she had had in raising a family without a father. After working this through to a point of relaxation, Helen retired to a corner. At this point, several group members observed that Peony was crying.

They were solicitous of Peony, but she would say little. Her voice was very tiny. I sensed that Peony blocked her feelings at her throat. A look at her body indicated a narrow chest, shallow breathing, and a tightness around the throat. Apparently, feelings were present in Peony, but she held them down through lack of breathing and tension in the vocal cords. I suggested that she scream. This is sometimes an effective way to break through and relax the blocking throat muscles. After a few futile efforts, Peony stopped with a look of despair. Some group members offered to scream with her if it would help. She agreed. We all screamed together. Then Peony screamed by herself, a loud, long scream that sounded as if it had been held back a long time. She took a deep breath, smiled, and looked pleased with herself.

Peony was asked about the tears she had shed, and she looked very frightened and became immobile. She could say only that she could feel the same kind of anger toward her mother that Helen had felt. Peony's voice was now stronger, but she faltered quickly and withheld her breathing. I asked her if there was anyone in the group similar to her mother. She said Josie. Then I asked her if she would be willing to arm wrestle with Josie. This was my attempt to mobilize both the anger and the breathing that Peony was suppressing. Arm wrestling requires a great deal of energy, deep breathing, and a strong contact with the other person through exchanging energy with that person. I felt that these requirements would help Peony become aware of her feelings and be able to express them more easily. In addition, her opponent had an important symbolic meaning, that of a mother figure.

Peony and Josie agreed to go ahead. I suggested that they

lie on the floor, raise forearms, look each other in the eye, and make noises as loud and as primitive as they could while trying to put down each other's arm. Peony threw herself into the fray with great gusto, and amazing strength came from her frail body. After several minutes of struggle, they stopped, exhausted. Peony looked full of life. Her face had color, her eyes sparkled, she seemed very content. She and Josie spontaneously hugged, and Peony returned to her place in the circle. I interpreted her relaxed appearance in several ways. It meant that the problem with her mother was resolved for the moment. She had made a certain amount of progress, indicated by going from tears to relaxation. If she had still shown some body tension, I would have encouraged her to continue working. Either the mother problem was not very deep, or, more likely, the next level of working on this issue would wait to present itself at a later time. Peony's whole appearance was vital. It was as if, through the physical exertion and the group support, she had relaxed enough to feel comfortable joining the group.

Peony sat for an hour or so while other events transpired in the group. At one point I sensed that there were several pairs of people who had not fully resolved their relations; I suggested that these pairs have lunch together and have two-person encounters (dyads). At this suggestion, Peony reported feeling terror. Her discomfort in meeting people directly had been tapped. Probably because of her earlier experience of screaming, she was now able to express her terror to the group. Her small-town background and orientation toward nature and "things" had not prepared her well for encountering people. I asked her if she would be willing to go to each person in the group and make some kind of contact. This was an attempt to bring her generalized fear of people into the here-and-now so that she could experience it directly, rather than simply verbalize it. She could feel the fear with her whole body and could differentiate the kinds of fear she felt with different people.

Peony agreed, and the group members and I stood in a circle while she went in front of each person and made contact both physically and verbally. Everything was going very well; she was feeling more and more easy with people.

She spontaneously hugged Josie when she reached her. Then she approached Philip, a small, kindly, middle-aged man. As soon as she reached him, she recoiled, covering her stomach, and looked terrified. She grabbed one of the women and started to shiver. I encouraged her to express her feeling, and she shouted, "I'm frightened. I'm afraid. I'm really frightened. I feel so frightened."

It seemed to me that this was the deepest feeling that Peony had yet demonstrated. The earlier ones had been important, and they seemed to be related to allowing and expressing feelings, centering around the chest and throat. But now her terror seemed centered in her stomach and seemed to reach a different level of her being. The situation seemed to call for a technique that would allow her to go deeply into this terror. I decided to try the guided daydream (Desoille, 1965; Leuner, 1965) in which she would fantasize going into her own body and going to the area where her feeling, in this case, terror, was felt. This fantasy method would allow her to explore below her conscious, verbal behavior and to build on the fact that the terror was localized in a certain area of her body.

Here is an account of Peony's fantasy in her own words:

Will asked me to lie down on my back, shut my eyes, and imagine myself very small inside my body. I felt very small inside a big cave with black tunnels leading off. I felt like Alice in Wonderland — there was a feeling of awe and excitement at being allowed in. I was trying to breathe deeply with help [I was pressing gently on Peony's rib cage to encourage deeper breathing so that she could contact the feeling more easily.] My jaw was moving a lot and I was still crying.

(Will) *Where do you want to go?*

I'm going down my leg.

How does it feel?

It's a bit difficult.

Do you need any help?

No. I want to do it alone. I want to be able to help myself.

Where are you now?

I'm in my feet coming out of my toes.

Is there anything under your toes?

There seems to be sand under my feet, it feels good.
Are you on the sand?
No, I'm going toward the sea.
Are you going to go in?
I don't know yet.
Have you decided yet?
Yes. I'm going in. I'm swimming slowly, I don't get very far, but I'm O.K. It's calm and warm and feels good.
Are you going to stay there?
No, I'm coming out now. I'm going back to my feet. I'm inside my legs and traveling upwards.
Have you brought anything with you?
Yes. I've got my sack on my back.
What's inside?
I don't know yet.
Where are you going to?
I'm about here (I put my hand on my stomach) in between the front and the back. I'd like to fill up the space and stop feeling backless.
Can you do it alone?
I'm not sure.
Can you use what's in the sack?
It's full of sea, it's filling up the space.
Can you feel your back?
I can from the outside — someone is pressing it on the left side [I was], but I can't from the inside.
Can you try to feel it from inside now?
I'm beginning to, it feels warm, and the front and back are together.
Do you want to come out of your body yet?
No, not yet. I can feel tingling down my legs, my knees feel strange.
Can you open your eyes and look around? [She hesitated. I felt that Peony, at this time, wasn't strong enough to be taken out of the fantasy.]
Would you like to go back into your body again?
Yes.
There's a mountain — can you see it? [Physical ascension helps give ego strength.]
Yes, it's here [she put her hand on her stomach].

Can you climb it?

Yes, it gets more difficult near the top. I have to breathe more.

That's O.K., the air is thinner there. Do you want to stay there?

No, I'm coming halfway down, it's too far to fall.

Is there something there?

Yes, there's a soft shelf where I can stay.

Can you see some way to hold in the air?

Yes, it's here. [Her hand was just above the "mountain."]

Would you like to come out of your body now?

Yes.

Do you think you can stand up?

I think I needed help the first time — my knees felt uncertain. I was helped up and was supported until I felt my knees were able to support me. I had a lot of sensation in my legs, especially in my knees, around the vagina, and in my hands — my body was extremely hot.

Will you look at each person?

I then met each member of the group in a way that felt very different for me, I mean, that I did not feel my whole being was threatened by them. That is except for Philip who was similar in stature to my father and held the combined identity of my mother and father; I still felt very afraid of him. After further contact with Josie I gained strength.

Would you lie down and now see if you can get up by yourself?

I got up by myself. Then I returned to Philip and felt unafraid. I hugged him briefly. I was aware of the increased body sensation and change in breathing. I felt I had come to life.

After she had completed this experience, the group showed its pleasure with what I had done by putting me on the floor and expressing affection toward me. When they were finished, Peony came over while I was still lying on my back and offered to help me up. I accepted. Then Peony pulled me up and hugged me.

The cycle was complete. Peony went from having to be helped up physically, to getting up by herself, and then to helping someone else up. She and Philip went to lunch together and reported having an excellent time. Later, she wrote:

I am writing this a week later, and my body is still feeling the change. I've laid my foundations, which feel like firm ones at last. The change in breathing still amazes me in the way that it really helps me to know myself. I feel very much to be at the beginning of living with myself, which means I am facing my adult self with a child's experience.

After almost two years, she reports a lasting change in her personal security. She has moved, traveled alone, supported herself, and she reports general stability and a continually increasing ease with other people.

EVALUATION OF ENCOUNTER

There have been several studies and wholesale lots of rumors about the effects of encounter groups. (For recent reviews see Luke and Seashore, 1970, and House, 1970.) It is difficult to summarize these studies; they are voluminous and cite many references. In general, they conclude that encounter groups can be valuable under some circumstances and not so valuable under others, a not unreasonable position.

It is technically difficult to evaluate the results of encounter (Schutz and Allen, 1966; Lieberman, et al, 1971; Bebout, 1971). I have spoken to hundreds of people who had their group experiences anywhere from 2 weeks to 10 years ago. The groups they attended varied in length from one evening to 9 months. Based on these contacts and on one study of my own, my impression is that the results of encounter groups are overwhelmingly positive (83 percent positive, 15 per cent no change, 2 per cent negative, was the result of our study).

When a group is badly run, the most likely outcome will be boredom, loss of interest, and eventual dissolution of the group. That damaging things happen to people in such groups can hardly be denied. Damaging things may happen to people when they enter any situation in which risk is involved. Some college students commit suicide; some businessmen have heart attacks; some athletes sustain permanent injuries; some automobile drivers get killed; some analysands kill themselves or others. The real questions are how frequent and how serious are the undesirable effects, can they be reduced, and are they justified by the positive outcomes? First, the emphasis on self-responsibility, when it is explicitly stated, thoroughly understood by the group leader, and consistently applied, converts apparently unfortunate incidents into important learning experiences for group members. Several persons who have been physically injured in groups, when confronted with their masochistic tendencies and their unwillingness to take care of themselves, have had their most important breakthroughs into self-understanding. Similar insights have occurred to people who have been scapegoated or widely rejected by the group. If the group does not operate under the responsibility notion, such people are allowed to wallow in their "poor me" roles, and they blame leader, group, members, encounter, society, parents, and so on. If the self-responsibility notion is emphasized, however, they are more likely to face what they themselves are doing that elicits constant rejection; this is usually important to growth.

If, as the group leader, I do not think that a person is strong enough to survive certain situations (frequently an anxiety more in me than in the member), I am free to give support. It is my responsibility to decide whether I want to give support.

Secondly, dangers in groups are being reduced by the new look at psychotic states, pioneered by Laing (1967) in England. Laing looks at psychosis as simply another state of consciousness, not in itself cause for alarm. "Madness need not be all breakdown. It may also be breakthrough. It is potentially liberation and renewal as well as enslavement and existential death." Dabrowski (1967) has called some kinds of psychoses "positive disintegration," and Silverman (1970) has done studies that help to distinguish the types of people who profit from this experience from those who do not.

Several therapists more within the psychotherapeutic establishment have also taken up this approach. Kaplan (1964) writes that the, "so-called symptoms, rather than being ego-alien manifestations of a disease process that has somehow gotten a grip on the person, are instead purposeful acts of the individual which have intentionality and are motivated." The notion of patients deliberately using psychotic states in an attempt to cure themselves is stated clearly by Bateson (1961): "The mind contains, in some form, such wisdom that it can create that attack upon itself that will lead to a later resolution of the pathology."

This work has several implications for encounter. As I believe more and more in the Laing hypothesis, and have more experience of seeing people through psychosis to better personal integration, I become less afraid of group members becoming psychotic. More and more, the message I convey to group members is: "If you choose to go psychotic, that is your responsibility. I and others will react to you in whatever way we wish. That's our responsibility. I'm not afraid for you to go crazy. It may even be a valuable thing for you to do now."Usually this attitude fosters a freedom to explore that can help some people. Persons in the process of choosing psychosis sometimes find that there is another, more effective way, short of becoming psychotic, to work through their problems.

When you become psychotic in a group, if I, the group leader, like you and feel so inclined, I will work with you to help you deal with the psychosis. If I do not choose to work with you, someone else in the group or someone nearby may. If no one wants to, you are usually sent home, to your psychiatrist, or to the nearest hospital, depending on your condition.

The notion of self-responsibility explicates the ethical code. "Shoulds" are imposed neither on me, the leader, nor on you, the group member. We are not required to do anything. We are responsible for doing what we want to do in response to one another. We are also responsible for dealing with the consequences of our behavior. If you feel that I, as a group leader, am callous, cold, incompetent, or irresponsible, you may choose not to attend my groups in the future. I may be unhappy and may elect to look at my own problems. But I am responsible. There are still no shoulds governing my behavior or yours.

The only exception to this last statement arises in the initial contract. I feel that, as the group leader, I should make my contract to enter an encounter group with you very clear at the outset. This is simply a way of making sure that you understand the rules for relating and have agreed to abide by them.

My experience indicates that this approach elicits the strong, responsible parts of people. When I ran groups in the more traditional way, being the "responsible" group leader, I noticed that group members were more dependent than I felt desirable. By making myself available for consultation at certain hours, by following up on all the participants to make sure they were all right, by providing a list of psychotherapists for each person to consult, by intellectualizing or interpreting a great deal in the group to keep emotionality low, and by stopping the group when some members were getting into difficult areas, I was communicating the belief that the group members were weak and incapable of dealing with their own lives, while I, the leader, on the other hand, was capable and would take care of them. Usually, I got what I expected, dependency and weakness. Hence my switch to the self-responsibility mode.

APPLICATIONS OF ENCOUNTER

Encounter as a style of life, rather than merely as a group technique, has been adopted widely.

The encounter movement is part of the larger social phenomenon embodying the various liberation movements, the renaissance of religion, and the call to honesty. The encounter culture encompases not only the use of the techniques associated with encounter and the human potential movement in general, but also those social trends that express the basic tenets of encounter: honesty, self-responsibility, awareness, understanding and acceptance of the body and of the self, and an appreciation of the unity of the organism. It would be exhausting and pointless to try to establish precedents or direct lines of influence between encounter and various aspects of society. Many trends consistent with each other and with the principles of encounter seem to have surfaced within the last two decades. The conglomeration of these I am calling the encounter culture.

Psychotherapy

Psychotherapy is the most obvious area of application. Many psychologists, psychiatrists, and even some psychoanalysts are trying encounter techniques in their own practices. Encounter supplements traditional psychotherapy. Encounter leaders have learned much from the psychiatric tradition and from Freud. Some basic psychological concepts underlie encounter, and traditional methods, in turn, can be enhanced by encounter methods, including non-verbal techniques, fantasy, dramatic methods, heightened awareness of the role of the body, a different conception of the role of the therapist, and new consideration of the roles of honesty and responsibility. More and more therapists are attending encounter workshops to experience this approach for themselves, and there are several workshops now offered for professionals only. I can foresee an exciting time ahead when therapists begin to integrate encounter methods with their own techniques to create syntheses that may be applied to psychotics, neurotics, addicts, families, adolescents, delinquents, prisoners, and other specialized groups.

While the encounter group was developed for normals and normal neurotics, it has also been applied successfully to psychotic patients. Here are some principles of application.

As the leader, I begin groups by assuming that you are totally responsible for yourself and that I am most effective when I assume as little responsibility for you as possible. I usually choose to assume more responsibility for children than I do for adults. Most traditional therapy involves the doctor-patient relation implying a less responsible role for the patient initially and only gradually giving the patient more responsibility. Generally speaking, I begin a group giving you full responsibility for yourself and only taking it back as I feel it necessary.

With certain types of psychotic patients, non-verbal techniques must be handled carefully. The use of methods to release aggression in patients whose defensive system is constructed around suppression may provoke anxiety. Patients with a very low self-concept, on the other hand, may find touching and strength-testing methods exhilarating and ego-strengthening. In general, encounter methods seem extremely valuable when carefully applied. This is true of their application, not only to psychotics, but to all populations.

As encounter is used with different populations, the ingenuity of the leader is taxed more and more. Encounter is not a limited set of techniques. Each group requires different approaches, and, as the leader, I must reach into my arsenal of methods tempered by my experience, to judge what will be effective. In a group of engineers, for example, structured methods at first may be the way to effect the transition from thinking to feeling; for a highly intellectualized group, many non-verbal methods are used; for normally aggressive, "acting-out" people, some physical discharge followed by verbalizing or fantasy may work; for a withholding couple, telling their darkest secrets may break the logjam that is their marriage. In other words, my aim as an encounter group leader is to learn many methods and, through experience, to become flexible enough to deal with any situation in ways that are appropriate and effective. For a description of many of the methods used in encounter, see Peterson (1971), Lewis and Streitfeld (1972), and Schutz (1967, 1971).

Industry

The T-group has long been employed in industrial settings, and the encounter group can increase the value of this application. Industry's use of encounter implies its acceptance of the values of openness, honesty, and individual responsibility and its recognition of the importance of developing the human potential. It profits both employers and workers to be open and self-insightful about themselves and their feelings toward each other. Labor-management negotiations are far more effective when they include the personal needs of the negotiators. Corporations hesitate to use groups more because they are reluctant to accept the possibility that by opening up their employees, they may precipitate the employees' realization that their own best interests will be served by quitting and going elsewhere.

Even acknowledging this possibility, using groups can be highly profitable. Finding people who are not happy in an organization and letting them go, establishing closer personal ties between employees working together, creating conditions under which employees are personally more satisfied, and setting up an organization in which employees are placed in the position where they function most effectively because their personal qualities have been considered, are all factors that increase working efficiency, personal happiness and fulfillment, and profits (Likert, 1961).

For workers, too, there are benefits. Encounter helps workers to know more clearly what they want, how much satisfaction their jobs afford, how they really feel about their employers, whether they would rather be doing something else, and what they must give up to their employers in order to obtain what they want from them.

Encounter has also been applied to business meetings. Typically, such meetings are highly inefficient. Important feelings usually remain unexpressed. Encounter facilitates the emergence of real feelings and the integration into the decision-making process of each member's contribution.

Theater

The relation of the theater, and of 20th century acting and staging in particular, to encounter has already been discussed. Imagine a theatrical production based on encounter in which the theater has a wall-to-wall rug, no seats, and a raised platform. The audience is arranged in groups of five or six and when the play reaches a point where a non-verbal activity is appropriate, the actors stop, and each audience group continues the play. They act in their groups. This happens periodically throughout the play. Audience involvement is almost total; every spectator is an actor.

Education

Motivation to learn is directly related to retention. The tragedy of many political-educational leaders is their failure to understand that by keeping students in the classroom studying Latin while the world explodes outside, they do not promote learning; further, they fail to capitalize on what could be learned readily, namely the fascinating social events of the day. They do not realize that the opportunity to learn about the social phenomena that take place on campuses — formation of subgroups, social disobedience, minority problems, development of leadership, problems of democracy, origins of unions, even the evolution of folksongs — is unique in our history. That is where the energy is, and that is where important things can be learned and retained. An educator using an encounter approach would find out where the energy is and would support it with people and methods that would best convert the energy into learning.

Several education innovations in the past few years are based on principles close to encounter: A.S. Neill's *Summerhill* (1960), Sylvia Ashton-Warner's *Teacher* (1963), George Leonard's *Education and Ecstasy* (1968), and George Brown's *Human Teaching for Human Learning* (1971). Two more recent books report the direct application of encounter in schools: Elizabeth Hunter's *Encounter in the Classroom*

(1972) and Marvin Rosenblum's *The Open Teacher* (1971). These books have in common the philosophy of forming the curriculum around the student; this is almost identical to the encounter concept of following the energy.

Another important application described in *Joy* (Schutz, 1967) is the use of encounter groups in the classroom and in the educational community. Widely controversial, these groups have proved generally valuable. Parental opposition to such groups should be respected. It is a great mistake to force anyone into an encounter group, including children of parents who object. I have found educational encounter groups most valuable when group members include a cross-section of the educational community: parents, teachers, administrators, school board members, and students. Such groups offer an excellent opportunity for closeness and understanding throughout the entire school system.

In an instance in which encounter was used successfully in a school system, first a general meeting was called to describe encounter groups. I asked for student volunteers and written consent was required from both the students and their parents. These were high school students. Encounter groups are new in educational settings and some parents are justifiably wary. Cautious parents are allowed the opportunity to see what the groups do for other children and the freedom to give their consent when they are ready.

The encounter mode may eventually become a standard way of relating in schools and an important part of teacher training. The use of these groups in school situations is one solution to the problem of relevance raised so often today in American education. An encounter group not only can uncover what is relevant to the group, that is, where the group energy is, but it can also help students to be more deeply aware of what is relevant to them on a personal level.

Childbirth and Parent-Child Relations

An encounter approach to childrearing begins prenatally with attention to the mother's emotional well-being, diet, health, spirit, and relation to her husband and others close to her. This care creates an environment in which the fetus can flourish. The delivery is preferably done with the father aiding the delivery as much as he feels comfortable doing, with a doctor available in case of emergency. The birth room is filled with close friends. Love fills that atmosphere into which the baby is born. The delivery is by natural childbirth, and the child is given to the mother immediately. The baby is held and given much physical contact and warmth all over the body; in this way the baby experiences total acceptance in a warm, loving world. Sometimes chanting or some caressing sound heightens these feelings. I am convinced that having the first contact with the outside world in this pleasant way has a profound effect on a child; it gives the child a loving, trusting feeling about life and people.

The love-oriented birth situation communicates that the child is included in the social world. Treating children as responsible persons communicates respect for their competence. This means letting children do all that they are capable of, the parents taking over only when necessary. The communication of affection is perceived primarily through touch and other nonverbal cues. Talking to the part of a child that understands is very heart-warming, and I have the feeling that, at some important level, the child understands. Baby talk seems demeaning.

The longer children are happy, the more they will be strong and capable of coping with the world. They are not natural enemies of their parents, lying in wait to take advantage of them (usually called, "being spoiled"). They are like everyone else, and adults can help them. Honest talk from their parents helps children build their self-concept. Children talk honestly to each other. They are natural encounterers — to begin with.

Religion

Many of the clergy have become involved with encounter during the last several years. Some feel that the encounter group offers a vehicle for parishioners to experience what the religious service only talks about. A feeling of the unity of all humanity is a common encounter group experience. Some basic tenets of the church can be clarified and experienced by means of encounter. Should you "love thy neighbor as thyself?" Most of us do not love ourselves very much. What happens if you "do unto others as you would have them do unto you?" Many of us feel guilt and seek punishment. Should we then punish others? How do ministers really help their parishioners with personal problems? They are not specially trained in that area. More and more of the clergy are turning to encounter groups for assistance.

A comprehensive study (Jud and Jud, 1972) of 150 clergymen and their wives lends strong confirmation to these ideas. The authors took these clergymen on a series of retreats using "the methods used in encounter groups and in the human potential programs . . . blended with the Christian concept of the nature of love."

In the Juds's careful research study evaluating the effects of the retreat, they reached the following conclusions:

> Behavior change was initiated and that long after the retreat (from four to ten months) the person, a significant other, and the data from the FIRO-B test indicate behavior change in over 90 per cent of the retreatants. This change was in a person's self-perception, in the way he expresses his feelings and how he relates to his fellow man. If on a three day retreat such significant help can be given people, how much greater opportunity does the church have — standing in continuous relation to its people — to train in the art of loving?

The encounter group offers a method for feeling and exploring many religious abstractions. When encounter focuses on the inner self, mystical experiences begin to occur. Combining the encounter group with the religious experience has helped me to elevate my aspirations for the encounter group. To look for the God in you, and to get in touch with your cosmic energy, have become meaningful pursuits and seem to redefine what I earlier took as encounter goals. Similarly, looking at interpersonal states in terms of energy exchanges is a religious experience for many.

The modern trend toward religious exploration is consistent with encounter culture. In an article describing the rebirth of religion at one large university campus typical of most, Hulbert (1972) observes, "For some, this search into religious origins is a means of seeking personal security or identity." In Hulbert's article, the campus rabbi said, "We see a turning inward. Half a dozen years ago people wanted to change society. Now they are looking more to find quality in their own lives." The trend toward religion is based, in part, on "the discovery that the ethical-moral system of America has ·fallen apart," an outcome of the loss of honesty in national life," and "a reaction against the nationalistic model of life," the lack of appreciation of our unity of mind, feelings, and body. A widely quoted scriptural text has gained a new prominence because we can now understand its profundity: "The truth shall make you free."

Society

Much of our culture is based on dishonesty. The phenomena of the government lying to its constituents, administrators lying to students, whites lying to blacks, businessmen lying to tax officers, and nations lying to other nations, have led to growing revolt. Encounter is relevant to this dilemma in several ways.

Many communities have felt the need to do something after confrontation and violence. What happens after a revolt succeeds? What happens if everyone is willing to sit and talk, to have a dialogue, to communicate and listen? The dialogue is likely to have real meaning if it is based on honesty. Self-deceptive politeness will not work. Neither will strategy and game-playing.

There is a widespread belief that encounter is a deterrent to the social revolutions. It has been called "the opiate of the people," the "reduction to psychological causes of problems that are sociological in origin." (Kahn, 1972.) Some social revolutionaries fears that encounter tends to make people personally satisfied and therefore complacent, that it tends to diffuse the energy necessary for effecting social change.

In my view, such an attitude is seriously mistaken. The revolutions taking place in the 1960's and 1970's are intimately related, and they include the inner, personal revolution, the one represented by the counter culture. The Reverend Andrew Young, associate of Martin Luther King and the first black to be elected to Congress from the Deep South (Atlanta) since 1900, has said that all of the revolutions must win if any are to win (Young, 1971). This seems to me an essential truth and one that must be clearly understood if the revolutions are to lead to true human progress rather than simply to the fruitless playing out of inner conflicts on the national stage. Personal fulfillment is of little value if we live in a repressive society. And it is of little value to create a free society if we remain prisoners within our own bodies.

The social revolutions of the blacks, women, chicanos, gays, and others, provide areas for which the application of encounter techniques is appropriate, both to make the social revolutions more effective and to test out the efficacy of the encounter method. How does the principle of self-responsibility, for instance, apply to groups that feel they have not been treated fairly by the government, by the courts, by the police, and by other elements of society? I would interpret it to mean that if these groups accept self-responsibility, as several already have, and feel that they cannot obtain justice through established means, they must do something else. Self-responsibility is often a prod to social action. I believe, in fact, that unfairly treated minorities have begun to rapidly improve their situations only since they assumed responsibility for themselves.

The social revolutions also test the principle of honesty. Does it really work? "Tell it like it is" and similar phrases, coupled with the strong attack on the duplicity of the establishment ("credibility gap"), are some of the chief rallying cries of the counter culture. I feel that as long as revolutionaries are honest, they have a good chance of success.

The application of the principle of self-awareness to social action is a point of controversy. It is through self-awareness that the personal revolution can contribute most significantly to social action. When radicals are self-deceptive, when, for example, they merely express their own self-hatred by trying to destroy established institutions, they probably will fail and will hinder their own cause. Should their revolution succeed, they will probably simply repeat the failings of the establishment they overthrew. As Norman O. Brown said (1967), "Revolutions are but repetitions," unless there is a change in people. Even Marcuse, a chief theoretician for the revolutionaries, in his latest book (Marcuse, 1972) states, "The emancipation of consciousness is the primary task. Without it, all emancipation of the senses, all radical activism, remains blind, self-defeating." He does not acknowledge the relevance of encounter to this aim; he admits to a lack of acquaintance with encounter.

It is probable that if you are self-aware, you want to change society. Aware revolutionaries know how much of their feeling is neurotic and how much is realistic. They know how content they are with things as they are and how much they want them to change. They know how much of their desire to help others is their own need — and therefore of dubious value — and how much stems from a genuine empathy. There is such a thing as appropriate outrage. There is a real world which could well be changed for the better. Being clear about our own personal statuses and their relation to that outrage in no way negates our social effectiveness. On the contrary, being clear leads to more success at changing the status quo and to real improvement of the society.

Daily Life

What about the application of encounter to everyday living? Certainly you can work on self-insight, on getting more in touch with your body, on being more honest with your feelings and more sensitive to what is happening to your organism as a whole. You can do simple things like being aware of breathing, muscle tensions, body pains, and illnesses to see what they are saying. Awareness can enhance the process of getting yourself together, of integrating your feelings, body, and spirit.

To be truthful and honest is a fascinating adventure. I find it a task of extraordinary difficulty. A lifetime of learning not to speak truth, combined with a real difficulty in knowing what, in fact, is true of me, makes living the truth a formidable challenge. The rewards are remarkable. I find I must relearn over and over again how really effective truthful living is. But virtually every time I am honest with myself and others, I end up feeling exhilarated; some of the body tensions that keep me from being fully open let go, and I feel a little freer and lighter, and breathe a little deeper.

Approaching a person with the intention of really being honest often reminds me of taking a cold shower. The anticipation is frightening, the initial impact, shocking, and the outcome, refreshing, cleansing, and invigorating. In close relations, I find that honesty is the key to turning the relation from attack-defend into mutual exploration and understanding. If I feel wronged by you, and you, in turn, are angry at what I have done, we can hurl accusations at each other. If, however, we start by being totally honest, expressing our hurts and fears, as well as our angers, we become two human beings trying to reach each other and to understand better what prevents us from being happier. We are now on the same side, not adversaries.

The practice of self-responsibility is likewise exceptionally difficult. The culture strongly encourages blaming others, fate, God, Western culture, society, middle-class morality, mother and father, racism, sexism, fascistic government. And there is some truth in almost all blame. Too often, however, blaming allows us to escape the more essential reality that we are responsible for ourselves, and that we are capable of taking care of ourselves far better than most of us ever realize.

My own evolution into living as a self-responsible person is also exhilarating. I feel I am just beginning to escape my reliance on the opinion of others. I am just beginning to believe that I can exist without any one particular person. This does not dehumanize me. On the contrary, I can love more fully. Becoming more self-responsible has freed many capabilities of which I was unaware and has freed me from wasting much energy blaming others. When I am dissatisfied with something, I pose myself the question: "What are you going to do about it?" If it bothers me, it is my problem; it is up to me to deal with it. Me. I experience greater clarity and, usually, greater effectiveness.

As I become more aware of my feelings and my body states, as they occur, life becomes more fulfilling and exciting. There is a whole underworld going on inside me, all of my feelings and sensations. I was so busy orienting myself outward, I did not even know that this show was going on.

As I focus on it, I experience more feeling, more aliveness, more pleasure; my outside contacts become more meaningful and more connected with my whole being. In fact, I suspect, I'm just beginning to feel what is meant by the word "joy."

SUMMARY

Encounter is a mode of human relating based on openness, honesty, self-awareness, self-responsibility, awareness of the body, attention to feelings, and an emphasis on the here-and-now. As a therapy, it focuses on removing blocks to better functioning. As an educational, recreational, and spiritual method, it attempts to create conditions conducive to a more satisfying use of personal capacities and to improving the quality of life.

Some of the historical precursors of encounter are the Greek Temple of Epidauras, Protestant and Judaic pietism, American civilization, and several Middle and Far Eastern mystical traditions, one of which is Sufism (a Moslem mystical group of the 12th century). In modern times, encounter finds its roots in group psychotherapy, psychodrama, T-groups, theater, dance, gestalt therapy, and body therapies. Encounter has had a phenomenal growth and has now reached what seems to be a period of consolidation and integration into the culture.

The theory of personality underlying encounter assumes that optimal growth is impeded by physical and emotional trauma and by limited use of the potentials available within each person. Several physical methods, particularly rolfing, bioenergetics, and the Feldenkrais method, are now available to deal effectively with these blocks. The body and the psyche are regarded as manifestations of the same essence, and understanding or treatment involves work at both levels. Psychologically, a person and a group are understood as pursuing three basic needs: inclusion, control, and affection. These needs are manifest in society, in the group, and in the personality and physiology of the individual.

Encounter deals with the whole person. It is assumed that the emotions of most of us have been suppressed by the culture, and that, in order to recover these feelings, we must become more aware of our bodies. Encounter stresses being open and aware and taking full responsibility for one's self, including one's manner of talking, feeling, reactions to others, and even physical health.

A wide variety of methods are used in encounter, including some borrowed from other approaches and many devised spontaneously to meet specific situations. No single method works for everyone. Having both a large repertoire of techniques, and knowing when to use which ones, contributes greatly to a leader's effectiveness. Self-awareness is especially important for a group leader.

Encounter has been assimilated rapidly into society; the encounter culture is emerging. Religion, education, business, government, theater, psychotherapy, communes, and some universities have been widely influenced by encounter groups.

Now seems to be the time for exploring the advantages and the limitations of groups and for seeking new directions for encounter.

BIBLIOGRAPHY

Alexander, F.M. *Resurrection of the Body.* Edited by E. Maisel. New York: University Books, 1969.

Allport, F.H. *Social Psychology.* Boston: Houghton Mifflin, 1924.

Anthony, J. "The History of Group Psychotherapy." In H. Kaplan and B. Sadock (eds.). *Comprehensive Group Psychotherapy.* Baltimore: Williams and Wilkins, 1971.

Argyris, C. *Exploration and Issues in Laboratory Education.* NTL-NEA, 1966.

Ashton-Warner, S.A. *Teacher.* New York: Simon and Schuster, 1963.

Assagioli, R. *Psychosynthesis.* New York: Hobbs, Dorman and Company, 1965.

Bach, G. and P. Wyden. *Intimate Enemy.* New York: Avon, 1968.

Barber, T., L. DiCarra, J. Kamiya, N. Miller, D. Shapiro, and J. Stoyva (eds.). *Biofeedback and Self-Control.* Chicago: Aldine, 1971.

Bateson, G. (ed.) *Perceval's Narrative: A Patient's Account of His Psychosis.* Stanford, California: Stanford University Press, 1961.

Bebout, J. *The Use of Intensive Small Groups for Interpersonal Growth: Progress Report of a Four-Year Study of Encounter Groups.* A paper presented at the American Association for the Advancement of Science Convention, Philadelphia, 1971.

Bennis, W. and H. Shepard. "A Theory of Group Development." *Human Relations,* IX (1956), pp. 415-437.

Bion, W.R. *Experience in Groups.* London: Tavistock, 1961.

Blank, L., G. Gottsegen, and M. Gottsegen (eds.). *Confrontation.* New York: Macmillan, 1971.

Bradford, L., K. Benne, and J. Gibb. *T-Group Therapy and Laboratory Method.* New York: Wiley, 1964.

Brown, G. *Human Teaching for Human Learning.* New York: Viking Press, 1971.

Brown, N. *From Politics to Metapolitics.* Atherton Lecture, Harvard, March 20, 1967.

Burton, A. (ed.). *Encounter.* San Francisco: Jossey-Vass, 1969.

Cannon, W.B. *Bodily Changes in Pain, Hunger, Fear, and Rage.* 2d ed. New York: Appleton, 1929.

Cartwright, D. and A. Zander. *Group Dynamics: Research and Theory.* Evanston, Illinois: Row, Peterson, 1953.

Corsini, R. J. *Methods of Group Psychotherapy.* New York: McGraw Hill, 1957.

Corsini, R. (ed.). *Current Psychotherapies.* Itasca, Illinois: Peacock. In press.

Dodds, E. R. *The Greeks and the Irrational.* New York: Beacon, 1957.

Dabrowski, K. *Personality Shaping Through Positive Disintegration.* Boston: Little Brown, 1967.

Da Liu. *T'ai Chi Ch'uan and I Ching.* New York: Harper, 1972.

Darwin, C. *The Expression of the Emotions in Man and Animals.* Chicago: Phoenix, 1965. (First ed. 1872.)

Desoille, R. *The Directed Daydream.* New York: Psychosynthesis Research Foundation, 1965.

Fast, J. *Body Language.* New York: Pocket Books, 1971.

Feldenkrais, M. *Body and Mature Behaviour.* New York: International University Press, 1949.

Feldenkrais, M. *Awareness Through Movement.* New York: Harper and Row, 1972.

Freud, S. *Group Psychology and the Analysis of the Ego.* London: Hogarth, 1922.

Gallert, M. *New Light on Therapeutic Energies.* London: Clark, 1966.

Gellhorn, E. (ed.). "The Emotions and the Ergotropic and Trophotropic Systems." *Psychologische Forschung,* XXXIV (1970), pp. 48-94.

Goldberg, C. *Encounter: Group Sensitivity Training Experience.* New York: Science House, 1970.

Goldfarb, W. "The Effects of Early Institutional Care on Adolescent Personality." *Journal of Experimental Education,* XII (1943), pp. 106-129.

Groddeck, G. *The Book of the It.* New York: Vintage Books, 1949.

Growtowski, J. *Toward a Poor Theatre.* New York: Clarion, 1963.

Gustaitis, R. *Turning On.* New York: Macmillan, 1969.

Haggard, E. and F. Isaacs. "Micromomentary Facial Expressions As Indicators of Ego Mechanisms in Psychotherapy." In L.A. Gottschalk and A.H. Averback (eds.). *Methods of Research in Psychotherapy.* New York: Appleton-Century, 1966.

Haich, E. *Initiation.* London: Allen and Unwin, 1965.

Hall, M.P. *Man, the Grand Symbol of the Mysteries: Essays in Occult Anatomy.* Los Angeles: Philosophical Research Society, 1932.

Herzog, R. "Die Wunderheilungen von Epidaurus." *Philological Supplement,* III, 3 (1931).

House, R. "T-Group Education and Leadership Effectiveness: A Review of Empiric Literature and a Critical Evaluation." In R. Golembiewski and A. Blumberg (eds.). *Sensitivity Training and the Laboratory Approach.* Itasca, Illinois: Peacock, 1970.

Howard, J. *Please Touch.* New York: McGraw Hill, 1970.

Hulbert, T. "A Renaissance of Religion." *UCLA Monthly,* (December-January, 1972-1973).

Hunter, E. *Encounter in the Classroom.* New York: Holt, Rinehart, and Winston, 1972.

Izard, C. *The Face of Emotion.* New York: Appleton-Century, 1971.

Jacobsen, E. *Progressive Relaxation.* Chicago: University of Chicago Press, 1929.

James, W. "What Is Emotion?" *Mind,* IX (1884), pp. 188-204.

Jud, G. and E. Jud. *Training in the Art of Loving: The Church and the Human Potential Movement.* Philadelphia: Pilgrim Press, 1972.

Kahn, M. Personal communication, December 23, 1972.

Kaplan, B. (ed.). *The Inner World of Mental Illness.* New York: Harper, 1964.

Keleman, S. *Sexuality, Self, and Survival.* San Francisco: Lodestar, 1971.

Kelley, C. *New Techniques of Vision Improvement.* Santa Monica, California: Interscience Workshop, 1972.

Kilner, W. *The Human Aura.* New Hyde Park, N.Y.: University Press, 1965.

Koch, S. "The Image of Man Implicit in Encounter Group Theory." *Journal of Humanistic Psychology,* XI, 2 (Fall, 1972).

Laing, R.D. *The Politics of Experience.* New York: Ballantine Books, 1967.

Lasswell, H. *Power and Personality.* New York: Norton, 1948.

Leadbeater, C. W. *The Chakras.* Madras, India: Theosophical Publishing House, 1968.

Leonard, G. *Education and Ecstasy.* New York: Delacorte Press, 1968.

Lerner, M. "Let the Nation's Leaders Meet With Encounter Groups." Los Angeles *Times* (January 25, 1972). (a)

Lerner, M. "American Precursors of the Human Potential Movement." An address presented at the Growth Center Celebration at UCLA, Los Angeles (December, 1972). (b)

Leuner, H. *Initiated Symbol Projection.* New York: Psychosynthesis Research Foundation, 1965.

Lewis, H. and H. Streitfeld. *Growth Games.* New York: Bantam, 1972.

Lieberman, M., I. Yalom, and M. Miles. "The Group Experience: A Comparison of Ten Encounter Technologies." In L. Blank et al. (eds.) *Confrontation.* New York: Macmillan, 1971.

Likert, R. *New Pattern of Management.* New York: McGraw Hill, 1961.

Lilly, J. *Center of the Cyclone.* New York: Julian, 1972.

Litwak, L. and H. Wilner. *College Days in Earthquake Country.* New York: Random House, 1971.

Lowen, A. *The Language of the Body.* New York: Collier, 1958.

Lowen, A. *Love and Orgasm.* New York: Macmillan, 1965.

Lowen, A. *Betrayal of the Body.* New York: Macmillan, 1967.

Lowen, A. *Pleasure.* New York: Coward-McCann, 1970.

Luke, R. and C. Seashore. "Generalizations on Research and Speculations from Experience Related to Laboratory Training Design." In R. Golembiewski and A. Blumberg (eds.). *Sensitivity Training and the Laboratory Approach.* Itasca, Illinois: Peacock, 1970.

Mann, J. *Encounter.* New York: Grossman, 1969.

Marcuse, H. *Counter Revolution and Revolt.* Boston: Beacon Press, 1972.

Marrow, A. J. *The Practical Theorist.* New York: Basic Books, 1969.

Maslow, A. *The Farther Reaches of Human Nature.* New York: Viking Press, 1971.

Mead, G.H. *The Philosophy of the Act.* Chicago: University of Chicago Press, 1938.

Metzner, R. *Maps of Consciousness.* New York: Collier, 1971.

Miller, H. Interview in the Los Angeles *Times* (January 23, 1972).

Miller, H.B. "Emotions and Malignancy (Hypnosis-Psychiatry and Organic Tissue Changes)." A paper presented at the American Society of Clinical Hypnosis Convention, San Francisco, (1969).

Moreno, J.L. *Who Shall Survive?* New York: Nervous and Mental Disease Publishing Company, 1934.

Murphy, G. "Experiments in Overcoming Self Deception." In Barber et al. (eds.). *Biofeedback and Self-Control.* Chicago: Aldine, 1971.

Neill, A.S. *Summerhill.* New York: Hart, 1960.

Oden, T. "The New Pietism." *Journal of Humanistic Psychology* (Spring, 1972).

Ostrander, S. and L. Schroeder. *Psychic Discoveries Behind the Iron Curtain.* New York: Bantam Books, 1971.

Palos, S. *The Chinese Art of Healing.* New York: Herder and Herder, 1971.

Perls, F., R. Hefferline, and P. Goodman. *Gestalt Therapy.* New York: Julian Press, 1951.

Perls, F. *Gestalt Therapy Verbatim.* Lafayette, California: Real People Press, 1969.

Perls, F. *In and Out the Garbage Pail.* Lafayette, California: Real People Press, 1969.

Pesso, A. *Movement in Psychotherapy.* New York: New York University Press, 1969.

Peterson, S. *A Catalog of Ways People Grow.* New York: Ballantine, 1971.

Plutchik, R. *The Emotions: Facts, Theories and a New Model.* New York: Random House, 1962.

Pribram, K. *Languages of the Brain.* New Jersey: Prentice-Hall, 1971.

Reich, C. *The Greening of America.* New York: Bantam Books, 1971.

Reich, W. *Character Analysis.* New York: Orgone Press, 1949.

Rogers, C. "Interpersonal Relationships." *Journal of Applied Behavioral Science,* 4, 3 (1968).

Rogers, C. *Carl Rogers on Encounter Groups.* New York: Harper and Row, 1970.

Rolf, I. *Structural Integration.* New York: Viking Press, 1973.

Roose-Evans, J. *Experimental Theater.* New York: Avon, 1970.

Rosenbaum, M. "Group Psychotherapy and Psychodrama." In B. Wolman (ed.). *Handbook of Clinical Psychology.* New York: McGraw Hill, 1965.

Rosenblum, M. *The Open Teacher.* Newton, Massachusetts: New England Regional Laboratory of the U.S. Office of Education, 1971.

Schutz, W. C. "An Approach to the Development of Human Potential." A report of the Continuing Human Relations Lab at Bethel, Maine (August 15, 1963).

Schutz, W. C. *FIRO (The Interpersonal Underworld).* Palo Alto: Science and Behavior Books, 1966. (First edition, 1958.)

Schutz, W. C. *The Firo Scales: FIRO-B (Interpersonal Behavior), FIRO-F (Feelings), LIPHE (Life History), MATE ˙(Couples Compatibility), COPE (Defense Mechanisms), VAL-ED (Educational Value), FIRO-BC (Children's Version).* Palo Alto: Consulting Psychologists Press, 1967.

Schutz, W. C. *Joy.* New York: Grove Press, 1967.

Schutz, W. C. *Here Comes Everybody.* New York: Harper and Row, 1971.

Schutz, W. C. and V. Allen. "The Effects of a T-Group Laboratory on Interpersonal Behavior." *Journal of Applied Behavioral Science.* II (1966), pp. 265-286.

Selver, C. "Sensory Awareness and Total Functioning." *General Semantics Bulletin,* 20-21 (1957).

Semrad, E. Personal communication, 1955.

Sheldon, W. *Varieties of Delinquent Youth.* New York: Harper, 1949.

Shepard, M. and M. Lee. *Marathon 16.* New York: Putnam, 1970.

Silverman, J. "When Schizophrenia Helps." *Psychology Today* (September, 1970).

Simeons, A. T. W. *Man's Presumptuous Brain.* New York: Dutton, 1961.

Spitz, R. "Hospitalism: An Inquiry into the Genesis of Psychiatric Conditions in Early Childhood." In Anna Freud (ed.). *Psychoanalytic Study of the Child.* New York: International University Press, 1945.

Spolin, V. *Improvisation for the Theater.* Evanston, Illinois: Northwestern Press, 1963.

Stanislavski, C. *My Life in Art.* Newton: Little Brown, 1924.

Tannenbaum, R., I. Weschler, and F. Massarik. *Leadership and Organization.* New York: McGraw Hill, 1961.

Thelen, H. et al. *Methods of Studying Group Operation.* Chicago: Human Dynamics Laboratory, 1954.

Tomkins, P.S. *Affect, Imagery, Consciousness.* New York: Springer, 1962.

Vishnudevananda, Swami. *The Complete Illustrated Book of Yoga,* Vols. I and II. New York: Bell, 1960.

Wesley, J. and J. Emory (eds.). *The Works of John Wesley.* New York: Lane and Scott, 1850. Vol. V.

Whitaker, D. and M. Lieberman. *Psychotherapy Through the Group Process.* New York: Atherton, 1964.

Young, A. Personal communication, 1971.

INDEX

A

B

V

W

Y

Z